Praise

Hope, Help, and Healing

"I highly recommend *Hope, Help, and Hea*[...] [an]y-
one who feels they will never escape the tr[...] [...]l,
hopeful, sensitive, and wise, this book offe[rs] [...]d,
and soul."

> —DR. GARY SMALLEY, author of [...]
> including *Food and Love*

"This must be the most helpful book on eating disorders there is."

> —LENDON SMITH, M.D., author of numerous books
> including *Feed Your Body Right*

"No guilt here, no hype, only a grace-filled glimpse, a true reflection of what
could be you. Trust this man because he cares with enough passion and honesty to get to where it really hurts and to help you (or someone you love) to
find creative healing."

> —GRAHAM KERR, TV host of *Graham Kerr's Gathering Place*

"I was deeply touched and encouraged that [Jantz]...believes people living
(or nearly dying) with eating disorders can overcome and be free."

> —CYNTHIA ROWLAND, author of *The Monster Within*
> and *The Courage to Go On: Life After Addiction*

"A practical plan for healing the wounds and growing into a rewarding life
beyond eating disorders."

> —ROBERT A. ANDERSON, M.D., author of *Wellness Medicine*

"Thanks, Gregg, for not only providing hope for those who are hurting but offering a way to turn their experiences into help for others."

—Dr. Lynda Hunter-Bjorklund, author,

speaker, and host of *The Lynda Hunter Show*

"Whether you are personally battling an eating disorder (as I did) or you care for someone who is, Dr. Jantz's book will provide highly informative and helpful steps to finding your way back to emotional, spiritual, and physical wellness."

—Kathy Troccoli, singer, author, and speaker

Hope & HELP
Healing *for*
Eating Disorders

A New Approach to Treating
Anorexia, Bulimia, and Overeating

Hope
& HELP
Healing *for*
Eating
Disorders

Revised and Expanded Edition

Gregory L. Jantz, Ph.D.
WITH ANN McMURRAY

SHAW BOOKS
an imprint of WATERBROOK PRESS

Hope, Help, and Healing for Eating Disorders
A SHAW BOOK
PUBLISHED BY WATERBROOK PRESS
2375 Telstar Drive, Suite 160
Colorado Springs, Colorado 80920
A division of Random House, Inc.

This book is intended to be a resource and help on the subject of eating disorders and to point the reader to the source materials that contain a more thorough treatment of the subject. None of the information presented in this book is meant to be a prescription for any kind of treatment, medical or otherwise, and reference to other organizations and materials is for convenience only and is not intended as an endorsement. The author has made every effort to present the current research accurately and assumes no responsibility for inaccuracies, omissions, or errors contained in the source materials. The author and publisher are not liable for misuse of information provided. The author and publisher are neither liable nor responsible to any person or entity for any loss, damage, or injury caused or alleged to be caused by the information in this book.

All Scripture quotations, unless otherwise indicated, are taken from the *Holy Bible, New International Version*®. NIV®. Copyright © 1973, 1978, 1984 by International Bible Society. Used by permission of Zondervan Publishing House. All rights reserved.

The names of persons who have come to The Center for counseling have been changed, and some illustrations are a combination of individual stories to protect confidentiality. Cynthia, Jean, and Kirsten, however, have allowed the use of their first names for their letters. Their stories are real.

ISBN 0-87788-064-6

Library of Congress Cataloging-In-Publication Data
Jantz, Gregory L.
    Hope, help, and healing for eating disorders : a new approach to treating anorexia, bulimia, and overeating / Gregory L. Jantz.
        p. cm.
    ISBN 0-87788-064-6 (pbk.)
        1. Eating disorders—Popular works. 2. Eating disorders—Religious aspects. I. Title.
RC552.E18J36   1995
616.85'26—dc20

                                                            2002007394

Printed in the United States of America
2002—Second Edition

10 9 8 7 6 5 4 3 2 1

This book is dedicated to Cynthia, Jean, Kirsten, and Sandra—
for their steadfast example of always fighting for hope.

Contents

Preface to the Revised Edition

It has been several years since the first edition of *Hope, Help, and Healing for Eating Disorders* became available as a resource for hope. Over those years, I have been privileged to speak to and work with so many people who have read the book and sought hope for themselves or a loved one. Their courage and determination have been an ongoing source of personal inspiration.

It is, therefore, with deep appreciation that I present this revised edition of *Hope, Help, and Healing for Eating Disorders*. The essence of the original edition is unchanged, but this revised edition expands and enhances the original. I'm particularly excited about the inclusion of Web addresses in this new edition. In key places throughout the book, you will find links for interactive Web pages where you can hear, read, and respond to new information and practical helps about eating disorders.

I have seen much good come from the original edition of *Hope, Help, and Healing for Eating Disorders*. May this new book offer the same hope, help, and healing.

Acknowledgments

It is a blessing and honor to team with Ann McMurray. Her gifted writing reflects my heart for those caught in the bondage of an eating disorder. I have the daily joy of teaming with her in the "Ministry of Hope" at The Center for Counseling and Health Resources. Ann also sees daily the clients who are touched by the whole-person approach. Together we witness God's healing grace. Ann, thank you for your consistent heart of service. Your talent brought words of truth and hope to these pages.

Many will be blessed because of the excellent team at Shaw Books at WaterBrook Press. Thanks to Elisa Stanford, who sees our vision and most importantly consistently supports us—you are a delight. I have the highest regard for Don Pape, for his ongoing vision of helping those with eating disorders.

I acknowledge each of you with deep gratefulness. May our collective teamwork touch many lives—because there is indeed hope and healing.

—GREGORY L. JANTZ

Introduction

"For I know the plans I have for you," declares the LORD, *"plans to prosper you and not to harm you, plans to give you hope and a future."*
—JEREMIAH 29:11

How do you measure hope? Who do you look to for help? What does healing feel like? These are elusive questions. This book is written to provide you with answers. Finding them will not be easy, though. There will be times when you'll feel like flinging this book far away from you—only to reach for it again. To find the answers you seek, you must have courage. You must have patience. You must have perseverance.

You are about to embark on a journey of discovery and a journey toward hope, help, and healing. Along the way, you will also discover a great deal about yourself, your family, and your faith. What you learn will enlighten and challenge you. It will illuminate dark corners and bring hidden things to light. It will provide moments of comprehension. Sometimes it will be painful.

When the pain comes, don't stop. No matter what type of eating disorder you have, facing pain with wise guidance yields strength. You are not on this journey alone. Many others have taken this journey before you. They have struggled to complete it and reach their destination of wholeness and recovery. Listen to the words of one of your fellow travelers:

You have given me the first glimmer of hope in many years. Your wise words are echoing in my heart, and I feel like finally someone understands and can help guide me through this to the other side. I feel strong, like a real person again. I can do this.

So can you. Have faith in yourself. Have faith in this book. Have faith in a God who holds your future in his hands. Perhaps you have picked up this book because you are nearly out of hope for your future. You're asking, "How can my life be different? I don't want to be this way!" If your supply of hope is almost gone, God has an inexhaustible supply, and it is his desire to give it to you.

THE WHOLE-PERSON APPROACH

Through my many years as an eating disorder specialist, I have wholeheartedly believed in a whole-person approach to treatment. This approach incorporates all the different aspects of your being: emotional, intellectual, physical, relational, and spiritual.

The whole-person approach is not a quick fix. It is a long-term, life-changing strategy for recovery and healing. It recognizes our complex nature as people and strives for health and balance in all aspects of our lives.

Perhaps you've been through treatment programs in the past that have proved ineffective. I urge you to try one more time, using the whole-person approach. I have seen its hope, help, and healing effects on thousands of people. Because I've seen it work for others, I know it can work for you.

No one thing can guarantee success for you. But when you address all the relevant factors contributing to your eating disorder, your chances for a full, long-term recovery are greatly enhanced. None of this can happen, however, unless you decide to start your journey. You must want to change more than you fear staying the way you are.

Your Emotional Self

The emotional aspect of your being refers to the natural feelings you have about yourself and others, the way you react to circumstances and situations. Feelings aren't always easily discernable—they can run very deep. The emotional self rides the currents of those feelings. It exalts and it grieves. It hopes and it despairs. It fluctuates with the tide of your emotional highs and lows.

Your emotional self is affected by your eating disorder. It is influenced by core issues from your past that you may not even be aware of. These core issues hold the keys to your self-destructive behavior. You do what you do for a reason. You feel the way you do for a reason. The reasons can be obscured by the very behaviors they produce. They are the fuel that feeds your present behavior and dominates your emotional self.

Your Intellectual Self

While our emotional self may demand more of our attention, each of us also has an intellectual self. It is the part of you that desires to grow and change, that revels in mental stimulation and learning new skills. The emotional self may feel the thrill of discovery, but it is the intellectual self that incorporates the discovery into who you are. The intellectual self can hold on to truth, even if the emotional self doesn't feel like it.

During the process of healing from an eating disorder, the intellectual self must undergo a housecleaning of old ideas, assumptions, and expectations. Some "truths" will need to be jettisoned, and some will need to be refurbished. The whole-person goal is for the emotional and the intellectual selves to complement and support each other in healing and recovery.

Your Physical Self

The physical relates to your body, to its physiological functions and systems. Many things can affect your physical self, from the medications you take to the food you eat. The whole-person approach will help you to take an in-depth look at your own body and how it is working. You will look at how certain specific physical conditions can affect and contribute to your eating disorder.

We will also look at how your body can function in the future. Nutritional advances offer hope to support physical healing from eating disorders and return your body to optimum functioning. Each of us has the ability to appropriately nurture our own body, providing health and vitality.

Your Relational Self

The relational aspect refers to your relationships with people in your past and present. Your relational self interacts with others and affects how you feel and what you know. It is in constant flux, affected by those you interact with daily, including yourself.

Your eating disorder may have dysfunctional relationships as a core issue. This book will help you look into all your relationships. The whole-person approach works to reestablish proper connections with others, mend past associations, and build healthy new relationships, including those involving appropriate sexual intimacy.

Your Spiritual Self

The final aspect is your spiritual nature. Your spiritual nature is where hope resides. It is the part of you that may be, as yet, unexplored. Don't let that stop you. Your spiritual self is a source of great strength and purpose. It has been my experience that those who recover from an eating disorder usually say that it was the spiritual that kept them focused during recovery and gave them peace and hope. The whole-person approach urges you to acknowledge your spiritual side.

The spiritual side is a casualty in the struggle with eating disorders. It can be devastated by the effects of shame and guilt over past events and the present eating disorder. Recovery is possible when you reevaluate and reestablish your spiritual relationship with God. Even if you have not had a relationship with God in the past, he has had one with you and sincerely desires for you to draw close to him. By doing so, you can come into contact with an incredible source of comfort and strength during your journey through this book.

WHAT THIS BOOK IS

Each chapter in this book will discuss one issue related to eating disorders. At the end of each chapter, there is a section called "Food for Thought." This section provides words of truth and encouragement. You can write down answers in the book, but you might want to keep a separate journal as well. That way you will have more room to write or draw, and you can keep the journal as private as you want. "Food for Thought" supplies tools of empowerment and gives you an opportunity to record your thoughts and feelings. Questions and related activities will assist you in integrating the material you have just read. (Often, what you read will produce an emotional, intellectual, and/or physical response. Be sure to record these responses, even if you don't understand where they are coming from.)

Writing something down on paper has a finality about it. Some of you may hesitate at the thought of putting down on paper what you have experienced or are feeling. I urge you to set aside any reticence you may have and actively embrace the "Food for Thought" activities and journaling. This method of disclosure will be positive for you emotionally, intellectually, and even physically.

You will also find three letters interspersed throughout this book. These are real letters from people who have suffered from eating disorders. These individuals want to encourage and strengthen you—healing *is* possible!

Finally, at the back of this book you'll find several appendices. Appendices A and B answer some specific questions you may have about eating disorders. Appendix C offers a questionnaire that could be helpful to you on your healing journey. And appendix D offers a list of other books that you may want to look at, including some books that are mentioned in this book.

WHO SHOULD USE THIS BOOK

If you are suffering from an eating disorder such as bulimia, anorexia, or compulsive overeating, this book is for you. If you know or suspect a friend or loved one is suffering from an eating disorder, this book could be the most precious gift you can give them. If you are a family member or loved one, reading this book yourself—and gaining an understanding of the one you love—may be the most precious gift you ever give yourself.

I strongly recommend you use this book in conjunction with others whenever possible. It is designed to be used in partnership with other caring individuals—a personal friend or professional therapist, counselor, or physician. Eating disorders are often pursued in isolation as a way to distance yourself from other people. By choosing to open yourself up to another person, one who is able to partner with you, you are taking an important first step to recovery.

WHEN YOU SHOULD USE THIS BOOK

You should use this book when:
- You can no longer live the way you've been living.
- You are tired of suffering in silence.
- You decide that hope must win out over despair.
- You decide that you are willing to open yourself up to learn the truth.
- You acknowledge that the choices you've been making in your life aren't making your life any better.
- Someone who really cares about you begs you to.
- You are ready to heal and desire joy.

HOW YOU SHOULD USE THIS BOOK

As you read this book, try to personalize it whenever possible. Put what you can into an "I" or "me" context. This book is written for *you.*

The "Food for Thought" sections often involve writing. For some, this will come as naturally as breathing; for others, expressing yourself on paper may be more difficult. To make your job easier, forget about grammar and spelling. Construction is not important; content is. Allow your thoughts to flow unhindered by concerns about punctuation or penmanship. There are no grades here, no extra credit or neatness points. The only reward will come from an honest and open heart willing to accept the risk of exposure.

There may be times when the words just don't come. Sometimes the scariest moment is the one before the first word is written. Don't allow this to stop you. Close your eyes and think about a piece of music or a song that conveys what you are feeling. If something you've heard or read comes to mind, write it down. Whatever you put down will be *yours,* whether you thought of it first or not.

If English is not your first language, write in whatever language you feel most comfortable with. Use both. Sometimes a word in one language conveys much more meaning than it does in another. In other words, use whatever tools you need to express yourself as accurately as possible.

If the writing just doesn't come, try drawing a picture. If you are writing and a picture comes to mind, draw it. If you are writing prose and a poem comes to mind, write it down. Don't restrict your response. Let your thoughts flow in the direction they desire.

You can decide who will see what and how much you have written. I believe that sharing who you are through this book with a caring friend or professional can be of immense value to you personally—and of tremendous encouragement to you on your journey. Doctors, counselors, psychologists, and self-help groups have all used the material in this book to aid those suffering from eating disorders. This is a book that can be of great value on its own, but it is especially powerful when used in conjunction with others.

WHAT YOU'LL NEED FOR THIS BOOK

To get the most from this book, you will need:
- A true desire to see the journey through.
- A quiet place and time to work.
- Something to write with. Try using a pen: You won't be tempted to erase what you've written. Whatever you write will have value. Let it stand.
- A journal or notebook to write and draw in.
- A set of crayons, colored markers, colored pencils, or all three.
- A readable, modern translation of the Bible.
- A variety of outdated magazines you can cut pictures out of.

For those of you who are taking this journey of healing, please realize you are not alone. Along with your fellow travelers, there is One who walks with you. If you have a belief in God, this book will be a faith-building experience. God is here to walk with you, to lighten your load. Trust him to be there for you, just when you need him. He has walked his own long path, with the scars to prove it. Trust him, trust yourself, and trust your faith in him.

WHAT THIS BOOK IS NOT

This book is not a magic text, designed to evaporate your struggles overnight. It is not a "cure" but a time-tested resource. There will be times when you love this book and times when it will be difficult to turn one more page. Struggle if you must, but keep turning the pages. Keep reading. Keep working. Keep believing.

It is not a book with "right" and "wrong" answers. This isn't some sort of test you have to pass. There is no prize for filling up the pages. The purpose of this book is to get you beyond the need for your eating disorder and to help you discover your truth. Sometimes truth takes awhile to find. Be patient. Each person's journey will be different, depending on individual circumstances. Some of the questions or activities in the book may not seem to apply to you. Please complete them anyway. You may come to understand or discover something unexpected.

FOOD FOR THOUGHT

To begin, examine your reactions to what you've just read and write them down.

1. If I could describe how I feel right now, I would say…
2. I also feel…
3. What I'd really like to do now is…
4. I'd really like to do that because…
5. What am I expecting from this book?
6. What am I expecting from myself?
7. The thing I'm afraid of most right now is…
8. Draw a picture of what you're feeling right now. It could be anything from a gallant knight on a mighty steed to a small child standing at the edge of a high cliff. Make sure you are represented in the picture.
9. Think back to a time in your life when you felt the same way. When was it? Why did you feel that way?
10. Now, pretend the picture you have drawn is a movie. What happens next?
11. If you could change the outcome of what happened to you before when you felt this way, what would you change?
12. What would you like the ending to be this time?

For a long time, you may have been doing all you could to avoid thinking and feeling many of these things. Be prepared for and understand that you will be reluctant to start delving into these sensitive areas. You can't change anything until you can talk about it. Being able to talk about an experience or a feeling will be easier once you have been able to write it down.

Be on guard for feelings of panic. Reading this introduction may even have triggered your eating disorder behavior. This is natural and should be expected. Panic will peak; strive to work through it. You are starting a journey, and that means leaving one place and moving toward another. This requires change, and change can be unsettling. Your eating disorder, on the other hand, is predictable, a known quantity. Your fear of change may suddenly make your eating disorder look more attractive or less destructive. Don't be deceived.

While you are focusing on the uncomfortable nature of change, you need to look again at the dead-end reality of your eating disorder. Yes, change and movement are scary and challenging, but you wouldn't have picked up this book and gotten this far if you didn't know—really know—that the way you are living is no longer acceptable to you.

The next chapter will help you understand the nature of your eating disorder and fully appreciate the inherent dangers in your behavior. Make the commitment right now to continue reading, in spite of any hesitancy you may be experiencing. The uncertainty you are feeling is natural. It is not a reason to stop.

It's your life we're talking about. Let's begin the healing journey together.

One

The Ticking Time Bomb

It had been with her all day long. A nagging, pressing dread clouding up a beautiful spring afternoon. Emily had hidden her anxiety throughout the day, engulfing herself in work to keep it at bay. Now she was headed home, five-thirty in the evening, and alone in her car. No one else was around to promote deliberate cheerfulness. Restlessly she switched from radio station to radio station, never staying on one for more than a minute or two. Nothing satisfied.

I hate my life.

Startled by the suddenness of the thought, her stomach balled up in a knot. Desperately she tried to push it back down. *Not now,* she said to herself. She was stressed, she was tired, and she definitely did not want to deal with it. What could she do about it anyway? It wasn't like she could really fix anything. Maybe if she'd gone back to school she could have gotten a better job. Maybe if she'd been pickier she'd have married better. Maybe if he'd been different they would still be together. Maybe if she knew then what she knew now, she'd have made better choices about any number of things.

That was then and this was now. Now all she had was her job, though she hated getting up and going in to work every morning. Now all she had was her apartment, the third one in five years because the rent kept going up while her income stayed the same. Now all she had were two friends left from high school who could only fit her sporadically into their full and busy lives. Somehow over the past few years she'd gotten left behind, and nobody seemed to notice or care. Most of the time, she worked very hard at not noticing and not caring herself. But today, it caught up to her like it always did.

Well, if she had to go home to an empty apartment, she might as well bring something along to cheer herself up. Her apartment might be empty, but her stomach didn't have to be.

Turning the corner, Emily started down the main frontage road alongside the interstate, brightly lit in the dusk with familiar fast-food signs. As long as she stayed in her car, she could remain anonymous. As long as she pushed the food bags into the far back floorboards behind the seat, she could stop at two or three places undetected and bring home all of her favorites. She could almost taste how good it was going to feel to sit in her apartment alone and really, truly, relax and forget for a while.

THE HUNGER THAT NEVER GOES AWAY

An eating disorder is a time bomb waiting to go off. Before you can do anything to defuse this bomb, you must first acknowledge its existence. This chapter is designed to help you identify whether you have an eating disorder. Specifically, we will look at anorexia, bulimia, binge eating, and compulsive overeating.

Whatever the eating disorder, its progression will have similar components. An eating disorder cycle begins with a general sense of unease or dissatisfaction. These negative feelings could be due to such feelings as boredom, sadness, anger, or resentment. These feelings may be brought on by specific events, or they may be ongoing, defining a person's general outlook on life. Even in the midst of a victory can come the unpleasant thought that the moment is only fleeting at best.

Next comes a desire to exert control over, to circumvent, or to override these unpleasant thoughts and feelings. Some people use drugs, alcohol, or sex. Some gamble, and some run mile after mile. For the person with an eating disorder, the act of eating is the cover of choice. The anorexic will use abstention from food to control these negative thoughts and feelings. The bulimic, the binge eater, and the compulsive overeater will use consumption of food to do the same thing.

The control over these feelings is fleeting. For the anorexic who abstains from food, self-loathing is never far away. The battle to not eat, when every cell is crying out for nourishment, is ongoing and intense. The need to consume excessive food is regretted and despised. For the bulimic, the binge eater, and the overeater who consume food, guilt and shame also come on the heels of that consumption, along with feelings of self-hate and hopelessness. Intense self-hate and guilt bring about an angry declaration: "I'm not going to eat like *that* ever again!"

Weakened already with guilt, shame, and self-hatred, the person with an eating disorder is well disposed to repeat the cycle again and again. The cycle turns around on itself as negative feelings prompt the eating disorder and the eating disorder reinforces those negative feelings.

Anorexia and compulsive overeating may appear to be opposites, but they are not. Food is their shared means for controlling that which seems uncontrollable. As a result, the act of eating, and its daily habits and patterns, becomes an ongoing battle—with the eating disorder sufferer caught squarely in the middle.

Eating Disorder Cycle

1. Feelings of unease and dissatisfaction
2. Desire to cover over those feelings
3. Use of food (abstention or consumption) as chosen method
4. Feelings of guilt, shame, self-hate, and hopelessness after disorder behavior
5. Renewed self-hatred over weakness
6. Emotionally predisposed to repeat the behavior

ANOREXIA

The smell of cooking filled the house, and Megan knew it wouldn't be long before the house was filled with people. People intruding into her room. People intruding into her space. People intruding into her life. She didn't care if they were family; she hardly knew them. They were mostly adults who seemed to look right past her to see only an image of one of her parents. What did they really care about who she was? How could they have any idea who she was? Her parents didn't have a clue, and they lived with her all the time.

Every holiday it was always the same. Endless, insipid observations about her appearance—how big she'd become, how tall she was getting. And then last year that comment by her uncle, spoken in a whisper when no one else was around, about how much weight she'd gained. She shivered in disgust every time she thought of it.

Megan truly hated sitting down with everyone else to eat. It was like she was on display. People she hadn't seen in a year felt it necessary to judge what and how she ate. What right did they have? It wasn't like she could tell everyone else what she thought of them! Being the oldest of the cousins, she was surrounded by messy little kids who smeared food around their plates and all over themselves. It looked and smelled terrible. And the adults were no better, heaping their plates with large amounts of every single dish. All the while complaining about how much weight they would put on between now and New Year's. They were such hypocrites. As if with their expanding middles and fleshy faces they had any right to comment on how she looked or talk about what she ate.

She didn't really remember when she'd come to the decision that this year she wasn't going to give them anything to talk about. She was only going to take as little food as she could get away with and then just spread it around, pretending to eat. While everyone else was stuffing their faces, she was going to remain above it all. Megan simply refused to join in. It was an excellent way to declare her independence from the rest of her family. She'd been trying out this newfound freedom from family and food for several weeks, and it felt great. She felt free.

A Fat Worse Than Death

Anorexia is, simply stated, starving yourself to death. It comes from an obsessive fear and a desperate desire to maintain control over that fear. The fear very often has nothing to do with food. Fear of eating or of being fat is substituted for a different fear with which the anorexic feels unable to cope. It might be fear of failure, abandonment, intimacy, or sexuality itself. By controlling something within her power—the intake of food and fluids—the anorexic allows herself the illusion that she is in control of her real fear. It has been my experience that this deep-seated fear generally starts in childhood and is manifested in anorexia by the conscious decision to severely restrict eating.

Anorexics still get hungry, of course, but their fear of fat causes them to control their hunger pangs. And when these natural feelings of hunger are squelched, the anorexic experiences the exhilaration of control. If you are anorexic, you will need to be very honest with yourself about your eating patterns. You may want to congratulate yourself on your willpower over food. You may be disdainful of those around you who are overweight, even deluding yourself into thinking that your abstinence is a healthy alternative to becoming what you think you fear—being fat, ugly, and unlovable. You may derive an enormous sense of self-satisfaction from knowing that you are *never* going to look as large as they. The terrible irony is that, deep down, you suspect you already do.

With changing social mores about what is and is not an acceptable body weight, it can be confusing to know what a healthy person should weigh. Add into that equation different body types and the hormonal fluctuations of adolescence, and often the answer to whether a person has lost too much weight becomes apparent only after the undeniable evidence of hollow cheeks and jutting bones appears. Following are five primary symptoms of anorexia, prepared by the National Eating Disorders Association (www. nationaleatingdisorders.org), to help shed light on this confusion.

- Refusal to maintain minimally normal body weight for corresponding height, body type, age, and activity level
- Intense fear of weight gain or being "fat"
- Feeling "fat" or overweight despite dramatic weight loss
- Loss of menstrual periods in postpubescent women and girls
- Extreme concern with body weight and shape

The desire to maintain a healthy body weight is fine, but the anorexic's obsession with food and with gaining weight is leading her toward slow starvation and death, not toward a healthy body. If you are anorexic, it will be easy for you to deceive yourself. The only protection against this deception is total honesty on your part and, wherever possible, the wise counsel of those who truly love you.

BULIMIA

Debbie couldn't get enough. It felt like a gaping hole had opened up at the end of her throat and no matter how much food she shoved in, it would never be filled. The rich sweets she'd chosen to eat first practically melted in her mouth as she hastily consumed every crumb. Eating them made her feel warm inside. Her face flushed with the massive infusion of sugar into her bloodstream.

Before her was a feast of all her favorites, though she ate them so fast she barely had time to enjoy each bite. She alternated between sweet and salty foods, offsetting one with the other. It never ceased to amaze her how much she could actually eat in one sitting. Before long, however, the craving to stuff herself waned as her stomach rebelled at the volume she'd consumed.

At the first twinge of upset, Debbie continued to eat. She knew from experience she could get away with a few more bites before the real nausea set in. It really didn't matter if she felt sick, because she planned to throw it all up anyway. There was no way she was going to allow herself to digest all of this food. Throwing it up would be unpleasant for just a little bit, but she was pretty fast at getting it all to come up. Debbie compared that to sitting around in her apartment for hours, barely able to move, suffering through waves of nausea not only because of the quantity but also the combination of foods she'd consumed. It was so much better to get it all out at once. It was cleansing, like she was vomiting up all of the bad feelings.

Once, she'd put off throwing up right away. The phone had rung, and she'd picked it up before thinking. Just her luck the call had been from a talkative friend. No matter how much she tried to disengage the call, it had seemed like hours before she was finally able to hang up. Now she knew better and made sure to turn on the answering machine before she binged. She made sure it was just her and the food.

The Dangers of Bingeing and Purging

Bulimia is defined as bingeing and purging. Bingeing means taking in large quantities of food, often sweets, in an uncontrollable feeding frenzy over a specific period of time. The purging that follows can be accomplished in many ways: self-induced vomiting, laxatives, diuretics, obsessive exercising, or even bouts of starvation. At least 60 percent of anorexics are also bulimic, combining the two behaviors into a condition that some call *bulorexia*. Unlike anorexics, bulimics are well aware of the abnormality of their eating behaviors. Anorexics resist the reality of their self-starvation, while bulimics acknowledge their dysfunction even as they are overcome by it.

If you are bulimic, you already know it. What you may not know is that your eating disorder is causing serious damage to your body and its systems. Bulimics on average tend to continue their behavior for about five to seven years before looking for help. Physical complications from the disorder usually send them into a panic, forcing them to finally seek help. One woman came to me after her esophagus ruptured, caused by induced vomiting following her frequent binges. Repetitive vomiting puts a great strain on the esophagus and larynx, or voice box, resulting in tearing and bleeding.

Another common complaint that causes bulimics to seek help is severe tooth decay. Stomach acids constantly regurgitated over the tooth enamel will eventually eat it away. I've worked with bulimics who have had their teeth capped two and three times. I remember one delightful woman who was trying very hard to be committed to a group I was leading for people suffering from bulimia. She worked at a dentist's office and had had her teeth capped several times. After bingeing and purging that day, she'd broken off one of her caps. That event was her turning point. That evening she came to the group with the cap in her hand, ready to commit to becoming well.

Another woman in the group had been binge eating for twenty-three years. During all that time, her husband and family were totally ignorant of her problem. She used laxatives to purge after her daily binges. She would get up in the morning, bake and eat a huge pan of brownies or other sweets, then bake again for her family. During the day she would take laxatives to flush her body of what she'd eaten.

The problem with laxatives is that they don't just flush out food. They also leech the body of essential nutrients, such as potassium, the fuel that regulates heartbeat. A bulimic who flushes out potassium or an anorexic who takes in no potassium will often complain of a rapid or irregular heartbeat. Eventually, this woman, like the singer Karen Carpenter, suffered a heart attack. This was when her family finally found out about her disorder. They were shocked, unable to believe what their loved one was doing to herself—or why.

How, you might be asking yourself, could they *not* have known? Because bulimics will go to great lengths to hide what they do. And when their behavior becomes too obvious, many bulimics will forego being around people rather than moderate or stop their behavior. As bulimics isolate themselves, food becomes the obvious substitute for social interaction. Food replaces other people as the source of comfort and companionship. Deception and avoidance replace openness and camaraderie.

THE BINGE AND HABITUAL OVEREATER

The party was still going full-swing in the living room, so Bob felt safe duck-ing into the kitchen. His wife, JoAnn, was busy getting the video set up for the kids in the family room, so he doubted anyone would be coming in. Half-eaten meals littered the dishes spread along the countertops, many still with forks and spoons sticking out. If anyone did come in and catch him, Bob could say he was just clearing up for JoAnn.

Quickly going from dish to dish, Bob gulped down several spoonfuls or forkfuls of each. He really liked the fried stuffing Judy had prepared and stood hunched over the bowl, carefully picking off the crispy sides. When he realized how odd it looked to have so much of just the sides scooped off, Bob downed two large spoonfuls from the middle to make it more even.

Glancing around to see if he was still undetected, he sliced off a large wedge of cake and ate it with his fingers over the sink. When it was gone, Bob washed his hands and his mouth, removing any evidence. He sliced another larger piece of cake onto a clean plate and walked back into the liv-ing room—with the "second piece" he'd announced he was getting when he first headed into the kitchen.

He'd worry about the consequences later. Either he'd work out a little harder or he'd just not eat for the next day or so. He used to do that all the time when he was younger. It had been a little harder to do lately, but that was just because he hadn't really put his mind to it. Tomorrow, he was really going to get serious.

The Best Intentions

Binge eating consists of eating larger than normal amounts of food at least twice a week for a period of six months. Binge eaters show a lack of control during a binge episode, just like bulimics, but without the purging after-wards. There is no vomiting or excessive exercise or laxative use. Binge eating is also known as compulsive overeating and produces feelings of disgust, depression, or guilt over the amount consumed.

Binge eating has no relation to feelings of hunger. Not only will binge eaters eat when not physically hungry, they will also eat past normal signals of being full. Binge eating is marked by rapid and isolated food consumption. Embarrassed by the amount being eaten, binge eaters will choose stealth and speed to accomplish their goal.

Binge eating appears to produce a lack of resolve to undo the "damage" caused by excessive overconsumption. Over time, a binge eater can become more intimate with food than with people, as food is used to give the binge eater sensual pleasure. This type of relationship with food brings social isolation, depression, and despair. Many binge or compulsive overeaters have lost hope that they will ever be anything but large and fat. They have concluded that there's nothing else in life except the pleasure food brings. The compulsive overeater's single most important goal is getting the next "food fix," turning to food as a calming influence, using food as relaxation and reward.

As the habitual overeater ages, he steadily gains more and more weight. It becomes harder to find the motivation and the physical stamina to lose weight. This is complicated by the drop in metabolism common with the onset of middle age. Many habitual overeaters consign themselves to gaining more and more weight as they head into their later years. The more they eat, the larger they become. The larger they become, the less able they are to physically address their extra weight.

THE SECRET THAT WON'T STAY SECRET

Whether a person suffers from bulimia, anorexia, or compulsive overeating, eventually the secret does manifest itself. Our bodies are able to tolerate enormous amounts of abuse, but sooner or later they begin to break down. Weight drops dramatically, teeth rapidly decay, the throat bleeds, and the heart beats erratically—or stops altogether. Twenty percent of anorexics eventually die as a direct result of their anorexia, and many more suffer irreparable physical damage. The stress of bingeing and purging also takes its toll. There comes a point when certain vital organs and glands begin to break down.

Eating disorders are emotional time bombs because all emotions are put on hold so that the person can concentrate solely on food. They also act as time bombs in our relationships. Other people cease to be as important as the relationship with food. Food becomes a secret friend or a hated enemy that no one else can understand. Feelings of alienation separate the person with an eating disorder from those who would help if they only knew.

Eating disorders also cause serious damage to your spirit and soul. The shame you feel about yourself and the way you eat, as well as the constant secrecy and deception, gnaw away at your inner being. The guilt and frustration of the disorder also hinder a person's ability to connect with God. The more you turn to a physical comfort like food, the less likely you are to turn to God for spiritual comfort.

Whether food is your bitter enemy, to be approached only with the greatest suspicion and caution, or your secret friend, eagerly awaited and constantly thought about, you need to put it back in its proper place—as neither enemy nor friend.

FOOD FOR THOUGHT

1. How do you see yourself in one or more of the descriptions of eating disorders above?

   Food is my enemy because…

   Food is my friend because…

   When I sit down to eat, I feel…

2. Why do you choose to eat the foods you do?

My "safe" foods are…

These foods are safe because…

My "unsafe" foods are…

These foods are unsafe because…

3. My regular binge foods are…

    These are the foods I have to force myself to eat…

    Create a "Fear of Food" chart. Draw three columns on a piece of paper. At the top of the first column, write "Foods I Fear." At the top of the second column, write "Fear Rating (1 - 10)." At the top of the third column, write "What I Feel"—that is, the specific fears you have when you eat or think about eating each food. For example, you may fear a food because it makes you afraid of physically gagging or you feel it is toxic to your body. Finally, set aside some time to fill in the columns to the best of your ability.

4. Do you use any of the following ways to get rid of the food you eat: vomiting? laxatives? diuretics? exercise? fasting? enemas?

    I first began "getting rid" of food by…

    I think I'll get fat by eating the following foods:

5. What percentage of the day do you spend thinking about food?

    How soon after breakfast do you start thinking about lunch? How soon after lunch do you start thinking about dinner? How soon after dinner do you start thinking about breakfast?

6. Do you feel as if you're better than others when you can keep from eating, even if you're really hungry?

7. When you look in the mirror after you've eaten, how do you see yourself?

   When I see someone who is overweight, what do I think of him or her?

   How do I feel when I can binge-purge and not gain weight from the food I've eaten?

8. Do you often eat alone?

   Eating in secret makes me feel…

   Do I feel that other people can't understand the way I eat? Do I care, or is it nobody else's business what I do or don't eat?

9. When you go out to eat with other people, you deceive them about your eating habits by…

   When I go out to eat with other people, do I order what I really want, or do I order what I want other people to see me eating?

   When I'm alone again, after eating with other people, do I "get rid" of the food as soon as I can? Do I then start eating the kinds of food I really want?

   Do I feel it's just easier to eat by myself?

10. The person who bothers you the most about your eating is…

    This person causes me to feel…

    Do I feel like I'm not being honest with myself and other people concerning what and how I eat? In what ways?

11. Fold a piece of paper in half. On one side, draw a picture of what you think you look like, or paste on pictures of people who you

think look like you. On the other side, draw a picture of what you want to look like, or find pictures of people you wish you looked like.

The difference between what I think I look like and what I wish I looked like is…

12. Look at yourself in a full-length mirror. Look at yourself from all sides. If you feel comfortable, strip down to your underwear and really look at your body.

Close your eyes and picture in your mind what you think you look like.

Open your eyes and look at yourself.

Close your eyes again, and imagine what you wish you looked like.

Open your eyes and look at yourself.

Describe below what you see in each case and what the difference is between what you see in your mind and what you see in the mirror.

The difference between what I think I look like and what I really look like is…

The difference between what I wish I looked like and what I really look like is…

IN THE RIGHT DIRECTION

FACING YOUR DISCOVERIES ABOUT FOOD

The one word that sums up your relationship with food is *obsession*. Piece by piece, year by year, this obsession has consumed your energy, your time, your relationships, even your own concept of self-worth.

Food is neither friend nor foe. It is simply an energy source for the physical and mental activities we engage in as human beings. Within the behavior patterns of your eating disorder, you have distorted food's true purpose and substituted one of your own based on your need to cope with the hurt and pain in your life.

To begin changing your attitudes about food, it is first necessary to admit that your present way of relating to food is unhealthy. But before you go chastising yourself for failing—once again—to deal with food in an appropriate way, keep reading. Your obsession with food doesn't mean you're a bad person; there are complex reasons behind what you do, and not one of them is because you are a failure.

As you continue, the complex puzzle of *why* you do the things you do will start coming together piece by piece, bit by bit. It took a long time to develop this eating disorder, and I urge you to give yourself time to recover from it.

Affirming Action
Memorize this affirmation statement: *The path to healing is worth the journey. I will have no regret.* Repeat it to yourself both silently and aloud. Write it down on a piece of paper and keep it in a meaningful place where you will see it often.

Two

Control or Controlled?

Nicole just felt tired. It was all she could do to get up and go to work every day.

She weighed eighty-nine pounds. All of the bones in her face were pronounced—eyebrow ridge, nose, cheekbones, chin. Her curves had melted away with the weight. When she smiled, her teeth looked enormous. Fortunately, she didn't smile much.

With coworkers commenting on how thin she was, she wore layers of clothing. She also bundled up, even on warmer days, because she was so cold all the time; she dreaded the onset of winter.

Lately, Nicole was having trouble remembering things at work. Normal activities seemed to wear her out and cause her a great deal of stress. She just didn't seem to have the energy to think anymore. When she got home every night, she curled up on the couch and slept.

Nicole could dimly remember what her life used to be. At first, the ability to forego food was heady. It made her feel powerful and different, especially when all her friends seemed to have so many things that made them unique. Nicole knew she wasn't really unique; she never had been. Then one summer she discovered she could say no to food when other people, especially other girls, couldn't. She'd never been particularly pretty, but after that summer there was no way anyone could say she was fat. If she couldn't be something positive in their minds, Nicole reasoned, at least she didn't have to be something negative.

Whenever she was angry at something, it felt better not to eat. Whenever she was sad or anxious, the thought of eating was nauseating. She began to compile a secret list of "safe" foods—foods she knew she could eat without throwing up. Her senior year in high school, she decided that carrots were one of her safe foods. She'd eaten so many of them, her skin turned a light shade of orange.

Ten years later, her list of safe foods had shrunk smaller and smaller. Everything about her seemed to shrink over the years, as well. The number of clothes she could fit into. The ambitions she had for her life. The people she called friends. Her physical presence. People seemed to be able to gaze right past her and not see her at all. She felt as if she were slowly contracting in upon herself. Sometimes, at night, she would find herself curled up in a tight little ball on the couch, amazed at what little space she took up.

Too tired to try to figure everything out, Nicole usually just closed her eyes to forget. Forget the way this had all started out, with that heady feeling of control. Back to the time when it had felt so powerful to be able to be in charge and say no to food. Somewhere along the line, Nicole found herself helpless against her fear of food. Being able to say no was no longer being in control. Now, Nicole was out of control, unable to say yes.

LOSING THE SENSE OF SELF

Few things are as frightening as losing control, feeling powerless against over-whelming forces. When overcome by events, we can feel swept up on relentless waves of circumstance that hurl us toward terrifying heights and bone-jarring lows. Each event is made worse if we have tried to stop it and been unsuccess-ful. It could be the sense of abandonment following the death of a loved one; no amount of longing will bring that person back. It could be the continual verbal battering of a family member; no amount of pleading will make them be quiet. It could be the searing memory of sexual abuse; no amount of wish-ing will ever make you feel clean again. It could be the careless taunting of peers; no amount of apologies can make up for the stinging pain.

The absence of control causes feelings of panic, powerlessness, and pain.

If the situation bringing about the loss of control is not fixable, some people substitute a different activity to control. This is the essence of an eating disorder. It starts with a feeling of control. Compared to the feeling of helplessness, power feels pretty good. So good, in fact, it becomes addicting. Eating or not eating becomes addicting.

Is food really the problem? Surprisingly, it is not. Eating disorders aren't so much about the food itself as they are about trying to take control of the actions surrounding food. People with eating disorders are involved in a terrible conflict, trying to control something that has control over them. This conflict soon turns into an unending struggle to get the upper hand.

For the bulimic, who binges and purges, the control comes from "breaking the rules" or "getting away with something." Bulimics feel powerful and in control when they can eat whatever they want and not suffer the consequence they dread—getting fat. If you are bulimic, you've felt that "high," the relief that comes when you've gotten rid of all the thousands of calories you've eaten on a binge. Getting rid of that food is like getting rid of shame.

If you are anorexic, you are taking control by saying no to food. By controlling your body's need to eat, and also its need to mature and grow, you are saying to yourself, *At least in this area, I am the one who is making the decisions!* The ability to have mastery over your own feelings of hunger makes you feel "high."

Obsessed with food but unwilling to consume it themselves, some anorexics will find enjoyment vicariously, cooking elaborate meals for others and relishing the meal by proxy. Their ability to enjoy food through others, but refrain from indulging themselves, brings about an enormous sense of power and control.

If you are a compulsive overeater, you have insulated your life from the world with food and flesh. You have learned that you can keep others away by being overweight. You have found that your one faithful friend is food, though it has now turned against you and you can no longer hide the pain.

Whatever your struggle with eating, there is another area of your life you're trying to control: your pain. One truth that has come out about eating disorders is that people suffering from them have had significant hurt in their lives. Studies have indicated that 80 percent or more of people with eating disorders have been victims of some sort of abuse—whether verbal, emotional, physical, or sexual. By controlling what you eat, you are really trying to control that terrible pain.

WHEN THINGS GET TURNED AROUND

Eating disorder behavior at first gives the sense of being in control, producing a feeling of emotional power. The greater the emotional power, the greater the false sense of control. We feel in control, so we continue the behavior. The more we continue the behavior, the more we feel in control.

By concentrating on the eating disorder, a person can postpone thinking about the circumstances or situation that made him feel out of control in the first place. He has no control over what is causing the pain, but he does have control over his eating disorder. This emotional power becomes the seed for pride. At first, he feels better than others when he can control his food. If he abstains from food, he feels stronger than others. If he binges and purges, he feels as if he's avoiding the consequences everyone else experiences when they overeat.

For the compulsive overeater, there can be a different kind of power. The compulsive overeater does not purge like the bulimic and therefore shows the outward signs of her overindulgence. The control taken by the compulsive overeater is the defiant decision to use whatever she chooses to make herself feel better. Even though she knows that eating food in that quantity is harmful, she willfully chooses to eat it anyway, declaring that she is in control of her own body, even if it means gaining large amounts of weight. *I will eat what I want, when I want, how much I want. It's my body. I'll be fat if I want to!*

The longer the eating disorder continues, the more this self-deception takes hold. People suffering from an eating disorder must create their own reality in order to perpetuate the behavior. This false reality tells them they are in control. The longer they stay in the false reality, the harder and harder it will be for them to accept the truth when they hear it from others.

The pride of this false truth distorts a person into thinking he knows better than those who are concerned about him. He may consider their concern really a jealous reaction to the control he now feels; he is in control and they are not. This warped view makes it more difficult for him to acknowledge the legitimate concern of others and to accept guidance from those most able to help.

Resolving the Pain

To make a lasting and permanent recovery from an eating disorder, a person must first deal with and resolve this pain. Unfortunately, not all treatment programs are set up to cope with the resolution of deep hurt and abuse. I know of a girl whose parents sent her out of state to a hospital for treatment. After six weeks, they got a bill for twenty thousand dollars and a daughter who was on four different kinds of medication. Her doctor's report said she had a "high probability of relapse." She was told to find a psychiatrist to monitor her medications. What she really needed was someone to help her understand her distorted need to control her life through food.

These feelings of control are frauds. In actuality, the disorder has control, consuming relationships, health, even time. If you ask a person with an eating disorder how much of their time they think about food, they'll say, "Oh, about 110 percent." They spend all their time thinking about *when* they are or aren't going to eat, *what* they are or aren't going to eat, *where* they are or aren't going to eat, and *with whom* they are or aren't going to eat.

Since you're reading this book, you are beginning to understand that your attempts to control food are failing to control the pain and the anger you feel. It is time to face the false reality of the eating disorder and realize the control you have given it. It's time to reclaim your own personal happiness.

EMOTIONAL FREEDOM

Can the person with an eating disorder be healed? Yes! There is something amazing that occurs when past hurts are resolved and the substitute of food is no longer needed. We've seen people change who have been bulimic for years. They never again have the desire to binge and purge. We believe that treating the whole person sets them up for long-term recovery and success. They take back the control over their lives that they'd previously given to food.

In order to recover from your eating disorder and from your painful past, you need to stop numbing yourself. You need to think about what has happened to you. It's vital that you remember as much as possible about past

A Thought from a Patient

At nineteen, I was raped. The rape left me devastated and angry, but I wanted to be a nice girl, so I refused to let my anger show. Occasionally, I couldn't keep my feelings under control, and I'd blow up or become too aggressive. Then I'd feel like a "bad" girl. Off I'd go to the candy machine to stuff all my insecurities and feelings of failure with chocolate. Whenever my life was out of control, I'd take control with my body. By always focusing on my body, I didn't have to focus on my fears, my failures, or my frustrations.

Through my bulimia, I thought I had found a way to control those painful feelings, to numb myself to the pain I felt. Instead of giving me a sense of control over my anger and pain, it ended up controlling every aspect of my life.

Dr. Jantz told me that it was time to stop numbing my pain and begin to deal with it. He helped me to take hope and courage from knowing there's a light at the end of the tunnel.

hurts so that you can come to terms with them and resolve them. It can be done!

One of the false realities perpetuated by the eating disorder behavior is the dread that something catastrophic will occur if you remember and concentrate on the pain. After all, you've constructed this elaborate armor to protect you from the pain. Maybe you even think that if you feel the pain, you will die. That is a lie; you won't die. It will be painful, though. But confronting and understanding the pain will bring about emotional freedom and allow you to grow in your pain.

There is light at the end of the tunnel. There is truth at the end of the tunnel. *You* are at the end of the tunnel. A *you* defined by your inner being, not your eating disorder. And so much more! Free from your eating disorder, you will be able to feel positive emotions, not just the pain. Freedom means a return of hope, joy, love, acceptance, laughter, personal insights, deep restful sleep, a renewed perspective on life, increased physical energy, and vibrant health.

Grow in your pain? Yes. Pain brings growth, and enduring the pain brings strength. Pain refines us and makes us better people. The apostle Paul knew this well and phrased it this way in Romans 5:3-4: "We also rejoice in our sufferings [that is, our pain], because we know that suffering produces perseverance; perseverance, character; and character, hope."

When we numb or cover up our pain, we do nothing to lessen its negative effects in our lives. We even compound it with the pain from the eating disorder. By denying the pain, we leave ourselves stuck in suffering and never move on to hope. But by acknowledging our pain, we grab hold of freedom—freedom to feel pain, and freedom to move on from pain.

With freedom comes accountability. When the person with an eating disorder acknowledges his pain, he also must acknowledge the ways he has devised to deal with that pain. While the pain may not have been of his own doing, the coping mechanisms are. Once he has accepted responsibility for the coping mechanisms, he is free to change.

Unfortunately, there is no way to acknowledge the pain without feeling it. It may be the first time you have really allowed the pain to truly affect you without a coping strategy. It can be intense, and you will need someone steady—such as a caring professional—to hold on to.

As you take back control of your life, you will rediscover who you really are. Maybe you have forgotten who you are. But God knows. I understand that you may not believe this. Your denial of the pain is not only fueling your eating disorder, it is keeping you from the blessings God has for you by enduring and going beyond the pain. How can he comfort you if you deny the need to be comforted? How can he sympathize with a pain you refuse to admit? How can he break past your defenses to touch your heart if you've walled it away with your eating disorder? It is time to work on identifying your pain and acknowledging the control it has over you. You will then see God's deep longing for you to rediscover who you are, who he is, and who you are with him. He will be with you as you endure the reality of your pain; he is there with his comfort and his love.

FOOD FOR THOUGHT

Use the following questions to begin looking at your relationship with food. Be aware, however, that these may be difficult questions. They will ask you to delve into the past and into your pain. It is best not to do this alone. Is there someone you trust with whom you can share these questions and answers? Someone who will accept you and encourage you, no matter what? If not, you may do well to look for professional help. A counselor can act as a listening, nonjudgmental ear. A pastor or trusted lay leader might also be able to hear what you have to say. If you begin these questions alone, be attuned to your feelings, and get professional help if you begin to find those feelings overwhelming you.

1. My problem with food is…

   What am I trying to control when I binge and purge?

What am I really trying to control when I keep myself from eating?

How do I feel when I stuff myself and then get rid of the food?

It makes me feel in control when I purposely don't eat because...

2. What kind of "high" do I get from bingeing and purging?

I get a "high" when I have control over my feelings of hunger because...

When I feel hungry, it's for the following reasons besides food...

3. What does my constant obsession with food keep me from thinking about?

What does my constant obsession with food keep me from doing?

When I can concentrate on food in the present, it keeps me from thinking about the things that happened to me in the past, such as...

4. Besides food, what other methods do I use to avoid thinking about hurt in my life?

Having been hurt by others in the past makes me feel...

When I get angry over what has happened to me, I want to...

When do I feel out of control with these feelings?

5. When I'm in control enough to get rid of the food I've eaten, or not to eat at all, I feel...

How could I be using the control over food in my life to make me feel better about the anger I can't control?

6. How do I use food to make me feel better when I'm feeling anxious or hurt?

   When I feel I'm in control of myself, I think of myself as...

   When I feel I'm not in control of myself, I think of myself as...

7. Close your eyes and think back as far as you can. Try to remember the first time you felt as if something was happening to you that you could not control.

   If this is uncomfortable for you, try finding a safe place to sit, like the corner of a comfortable couch or a chair. Ask a trusted friend to sit near you. Try hugging a pillow to yourself to help you feel safe and anchored. Tell yourself that it's okay to remember this.

   Where are you?

   What is happening to you?

   Why do you feel as if you have no control over what is happening to you or around you?

   What events or circumstances have control over you?

   Does another person have power over you?

   How does being in this situation make you feel?

   What do you think it means to be in control?

   When did you first say that you'd never let yourself feel like this again?

8. Come back to the present. Remembering what you felt back then, when have you felt that same way since?

How did I feel when that same loss of control happened to me again?

I felt helpless in that situation because...

Why did I feel powerless to change what was happening?

When I can eat anything I want, or keep from eating, it gives me a sense of power over...

How does that restored sense of power "make up" for the times in my life when I felt powerless?

9. Write down one or two words or phrases that describe how you feel before, during, and after you binge and purge. Or jot down word images of how you feel when you can keep yourself from eating.

Write down the feelings you experience when you think about being fat.

IN THE RIGHT DIRECTION

THINKING ABOUT YOUR RECOVERY

Recovery involves risk. By honestly answering the questions in this chapter, you've had to put your numbness on hold and begin to feel emotions you've been avoiding. I know that these questions *hurt*, but you need to give yourself permission to feel the pain. This time, however, the pain you feel will help lead toward your healing.

The sleeper must be awakened. The time has come for you to wake up out of the nightmare your eating disorder has become, and start to really *feel* the world again. Yes, there will be pain to reexperience on your journey. But there will also be joy, love, true happiness, and, maybe, peace. The choice is yours.

AFFIRMING ACTION

I choose to take hold of my pain—to strengthen me, not weaken me. Think about this statement. Go over it in your mind and claim it for your own. Accept the responsibility for what it means in your life. It is okay to cry and be afraid, but don't let that stop you. Work through your fear and find a safe place to experience your pain. What you feel you can heal. You can walk through it.

Three

When Families Unravel

Carl cringed, hearing the raised voices through the front door as he approached the house. Part of him wanted to turn around right there and run far away. But he couldn't. He'd get in trouble for coming home late. Heart sinking, he opened the door and stepped into the battle zone known as Home. His father and older brother were in the midst of another fight, yelling at each other at the top of their lungs. His mother was nowhere to be seen, probably hiding out in the kitchen. His father and brother were too busy hurling insults at each other to notice him passing by the den. They'd be sure to notice if he went down the hall to his room, so he decided to take refuge with his mother.

Sure enough, there she was in the kitchen, furiously stirring up a peace offering. As if the smell of a freshly baked cake could chase all the ugliness in the house away. Carl's eyes met hers. Silently they agreed to talk about something—anything—else.

"What're we having for dinner?" he asked, lifting the lid of the pot on the stove. The rich smell of spaghetti sauce filled his nose. The more his brother and father fought, the more his mother cooked. Carl wasn't planning to leave the kitchen, not with the two of them at each other full tilt, so he helped his mother set the kitchen table. The kitchen was their unspoken haven; the fights never seemed to intrude there.

In the den, the fight was reaching a crescendo. As Carl filled up his glass with milk, he heard the front door slam and his father swear loudly. For a moment, the house was silent. Carl and his mother looked at each other, waiting. They were putting dinner on the table when his father burst into the kitchen and shouted, "Let's eat!"

His face was red, and he was breathing in a deep, deliberate way. He attacked the serving dishes, heaping food onto his plate. "What are you staring at?" he snapped at Carl. "Just eat your dinner!" Carl complied. He knew his father would eat quickly and then disappear into his study for the rest of the evening. Carl would stay in the kitchen with his mother, having a second, sometimes even a third, helping. She would ask about his day, how school was going, and feel good that at least someone was grateful for all of her hard work. After dinner, Carl would help her clean up, and she would hug him tightly and tell him what a good son he was.

It was safe in the kitchen. It was warm in the kitchen. And there was always the cake.

ALL IN THE FAMILY

The key to an eating disorder lies in relationships. For most people, those relationships lie within the family. The behaviors surrounding an eating disorder are the result of a relationship—perhaps several relationships—tilting off the mark. You may be able to pinpoint immediately where and when your life diverged from what you wanted it to be. Or maybe you can trace a slow slide from the ideal to the real.

You would probably rather not take the time to discover the truth about your family, or about yourself and your family. You would rather just forget it. But your eating disorder ties you to that problematic relationship. Your choices are simple: You can choose to continue with your eating disorder, or you can choose to examine your relationships and understand how they are affecting your behavior.

This rediscovery is not an easy process. It will require you to reconsider your childhood with an adult's point of view. The purpose is to understand how your family interacted and how that interaction is affecting you now—to understand your relationships, but then to forgive and move forward.

Just because you have left the family doesn't mean the family has left you. No matter where you go, the family continues to influence who you are and how you approach life.

Even after a person has come to understand how his family affects him, if he merely stops there, it will not be far enough. With understanding can come deep pain and an acute sense of betrayal and indescribable loss. This is not the place to stop. There is a place further on, where forgiveness lies. It is a place far removed from blame. Blame only fuels an eating disorder. Forgiveness dilutes its power.

FAMILY PATTERNS

Some characteristics are common to families that produce members with eating disorders. The following characteristics are modified from the Family System Continuum, devised by Wayne Kritsberg, author of *The Adult Children of Alcoholics Syndrome.*

- Many rigid rules, often contradicting each other or applied inconsistently within the family.
- Rigid roles within the family, where each member is defined in a hierarchical structure, with those in power defining the roles of those beneath them, to their own personal advantage.
- Family secrets, with explicit or implied negative consequences for "betraying the family."
- Resists outsiders entering the family unit, due in large part to the need to keep the family secrets. The more people that know, the harder it is to keep the secrets. In addition, outsiders may question the way the family system operates.
- Very serious, little laughter or lightheartedness. Generally this somber, tense family demeanor is set by whichever member holds power within the family.

- Lack of respect for personal boundaries, where respect for others is withheld from subservient family members. Members cease to be individuals within the family system and are not respected as such.
- Disproportionate connection to the family. Even after a member has left the immediate family, the family is still the central focus of that person's life and behaviors.
- Resistant to change. This family avoids introspection and self-examination. Family members are not open to admitting fault.
- This family is fragmented. Each member has a distinct role that does not change or blend with the others.

Healthy families also have distinctive characteristics:

- Few rigid rules, derived from a common set of values. Each family member is given opportunity to question these rules and seek modification, as appropriate.
- Flexible roles, with family members allowed to grow and change.
- Open and honest about the family—a deliberate decision to acknowledge faults and avoid the oppression of family secrets, while still respecting the privacy of family members, as appropriate.
- Outsiders are welcomed into the family and considered special. Outsiders are viewed as a way to expand the love of the family to others.
- This family enjoys laughter and has an ability to laugh at itself. Individual characteristics of family members are considered endearing, and laughter is always done *with* the person, never at the person's expense.
- Members have the right to personal privacy and the right to develop an individual sense of self. Personal privacy and self-awareness are not viewed as hostile to the family unit; instead, they are encouraged and embraced as contributing to the strength of the family.

- Members have a sense of being part of the family, but they are allowed to venture out and operate outside the boundaries of the family. Members are trusted to adhere to core family beliefs and values, whether within the confines of the family or out.
- Conflict between members is allowed, acknowledged, and constructively resolved.
- The family continues to change and grow as individual members change and grow. This change is anticipated, accepted, and appreciated.
- Each family member has a sense of, and takes pleasure in, being an individual and being a member of the family. The family provides the support structure for expanding each member as an individual.[1]

Your home may have been a place where punishment was dealt out quickly, strictly, and often physically. Guilt or shame may have been used to control your behavior. If you came from such a home environment, you may have been expected to act like a little adult. If you were the oldest child, you may have been given the responsibility of raising the younger siblings, short-circuiting your own childhood. Faced with a home where there were strict rules, rigid discipline, and perfectionistic behavior, you may not have been allowed to function as a normal child—safe, carefree, and sure that you were loved.

Whatever your specific eating disorder, you will need to look back at yourself and your family relationships and come to some conclusions about where you came from and who you are now.

This look at yourself and your family must be done honestly, thoroughly, and without blame. So much of what was done in the past is set; it must be accepted for what it is and how it affects you today. If the result of this search stops at anger, resentment, and blame, it will only fuel your eating disorder. The goal is understanding, not retribution.

Parenting and the Past

If you are a parent yourself, you will need to evaluate your own parenting style and come to some conclusions as to its effectiveness with your own children. Reviewing what you're doing with your own kids can help you to remember what your parents did to you.

Look especially at how you respond under stress. It is in those moments that we are most apt to react with patterns we learned from our parents. How often have you reacted in anger to another family member, only to stop and realize you were acting just like one of your parents?

If, as a child, you learned improper skills from your own parents, you came into parenting at a disadvantage. Often, styles of parenting stretch back through several generations. The parenting skills used by your own mother and father may have been learned from their parents. It's not easy to identify and modify these parenting cycles. Your own parents may have been doing their best, as they understood it.

The Perfect Sponge

The child who develops an eating disorder is often the sponge of the family, absorbing and retaining all the toxic waste—the dysfunction—of the family.

- One son sees another being rebellious and vows to achieve perfection in order to make up for his brother's behavior and to avoid the same harsh punishment his brother receives.
- A daughter sees disparity in the way she is treated versus her brother, and she inwardly begins to despise her femininity.
- A child within the family sees the way Mom responds to her own weight and, as a result, begins to equate body fat with self-loathing.

Usually, it is not the outwardly rebellious child in the family who develops an eating disorder. The demonstrative child has ample ways to communicate frustration, dissatisfaction, and even rage. The quiet child, however, does not overtly thwart the power structure but takes on responsibility for the woes of the family. The behavior of the eating disorder acts as a squeezing mechanism when the sponge becomes painfully full.

A Cry for Help

There is another aspect of families and eating disorders that needs to be addressed. You may actually be using your eating disorder to gain the attention of your family. If you suspect that might be the case, ask yourself the following questions:

- What do I want my family to know?
- Why have I chosen this eating disorder to communicate my frustration with my family?
- If I did not have this eating disorder, what other way would I choose to make myself heard?
- Why do I think that no one listens to me?
- What will I do if someone does listen?
- Am I willing to stop my eating disorder?
- Am I willing to continue with my eating disorder to take the focus off of something else painful that is happening in my family?

Your eating disorder may have started as a way to deal with pain or frustration or anger or loss, but it has a way of taking on a life all its own. There is only one way to defuse its ability to control you. It's time to deal with your pain.

FOOD FOR THOUGHT

Take a minute to think about your family. If you have any pictures taken when you were growing up, get them. Take a long look at them and try to remember what it was like to be the child you were back then. Can you put yourself back into those pictures, feel what you were feeling then?

If you have no pictures to jog your memory, then let your mind supply the images. Find a comfortable place to sit or lie down, and let your mind run backward, taking you further and further into the past. Stop anywhere you want along the way and look.

1. If you still have a favorite doll, blanket, or memento from your past, go get it and hold it. Discover what it's telling you. Write it down.

2. Now draw a picture of your family. (It doesn't have to be a Renoir— just draw stick figures if you need to—but be sure to draw faces and expressions.) If you are of an artistic bent, put in details.

3. Now, looking at any pictures or mementos you may have and at your drawing, think about these next questions and write your answers in your journal.

    If there were one word to describe my family, what would it be, and why?

    How did my mother and father get along with one another? How did my siblings get along with each other?

4. When I was growing up, I learned that God was…

5. How did I get along with my mother? What was my mother like?

    My mother would always…

    What did she expect from me growing up? My mother taught me to…

    My mother's moods were…

    Was my mother concerned about her weight when she was growing up?

    When my mother was stressed, she would…

My mother taught me that food was…

My mother taught me that diets were…

How much time did my mother spend worrying about how much I weighed?

6. What was my father like?

    How did I get along with my father?

    My father expected me to…

    When I was alone with my father, I felt…

    My father's job caused him to…

    How much time did my father spend around the house? When he was home, was he really home? When my father was home, he spent most of his time…

    Did my father and I talk a lot? What did we talk about? My father expected me to…

    My inner conflicts about my father were…

    Did some of the things my father wanted to talk about make me feel uncomfortable? Why?

    Did I ever wish he'd talk to my mother instead of to me?

7. When I was growing up, the rules for my family were:

    When did I have trouble living up to those rules?

    As a child I got in trouble for…

8. Did I ever wonder if my mother or father really loved me?

9. Are there any abusive events that took place in my childhood? What are they?

10. What did I want to say to my parents, but could only say in my head?

   If I could say those things to them today, I would say…

11. Chances are, when you were growing up, your parents used to say the same things over and over to you, especially when they weren't too happy with you. Think back to what those pat phrases or speeches were, and write them down.

12. If you are a parent, take some time and think about some of the phrases you use with your own children. Think specifically about those things you say to them when you're stressed or angry. Compare that list to a list of things your parents said to you.

   Even if you are not a parent, surely you remember things that you swore you'd never say or do to your own kids. Write those down. Compare lists.

IN THE RIGHT DIRECTION

FACING THE PAST

Dredging up the past can be compared to dredging up a canal or waterway. You get all sorts of mud, muck, slime—and maybe a piece of gold. The memories of childhood have filtered down to the bottom of your mind: the good and the bad, the treasure and the trash, intermingled together over time. You can't retrieve the one without disturbing the other. Be prepared for some murky water as you sift through your memories to find the answers you need for your recovery.

If you're like most people, revealing the truth about your family probably makes you feel panicked. One of the lessons most families teach early on is, "Keep the secrets." Revealing them can seem like betrayal.

Understanding who you are, the family you came out of, and how your family affects you today is not betrayal. The betrayal would be if you continued to allow the secrets of the past to destroy you in the present.

Somewhere inside of you is the child you were, bewildered over events beyond your control, hurting and confused over behavior you couldn't begin to understand back then. Keeping the secrets means keeping that child locked away in time, never able to receive the love you needed, never able to put the pieces together in a pattern you can understand.

AFFIRMING ACTION

Truth is an extremely powerful entity. It defines reality and provides the power to understand, to accept, and to change.

In your search for answers, in your journey toward recovery, don't lose sight of this fundamental truth: You are not alone. God knows your truth and loves you. Your truth is safe in his love. Pray this prayer whenever the pain of your truth threatens to overwhelm you:

Safe within your love, O God, I choose to seek and face my truth.

Four

The Hidden Shadow
of Abuse

The anniversary party was in full swing. The sounds of conversation, laughter, and the clanking of silverware on dinner plates hovered just over the top of the soft swing music playing from the band on the stage. Kate peered out from the doorway to the storage closet. She'd volunteered to check how many more bottles of sparkling wine were chilling in the borrowed ice chests. If it hadn't been this excuse, she would have offered to take the garbage out—anything to be out of public view for a minute to compose herself. Besides, there was no point in even trying to eat something herself. The whole evening was far too stressful to add a sour stomach to a sour mood.

She opened the doorway a crack to see her parents at the head table. There he was, holding court, drinking up not only the wine but the good wishes of the assembled guests. Celebrating fifty years of marriage. Gold paper bells and ivory love birds as table centerpieces. Outdated photos were lined up on a covered folding table, carefully selected to portray a loving, close marriage. Baby pictures of Kate and her brothers and sister—a happy, normal family. It was all she could do to keep from screaming, *"Liar!"*

Kate wasn't very old when she realized that Home Daddy and Other Daddy were two completely different people. Other Daddy bragged about how great his children were. Home Daddy generally ignored his children except to snap at them when they'd done something wrong. Other Daddy hugged her gently and patted her on the back. Home Daddy rarely hugged her; when he did, it just didn't feel right. Other Daddy spoke calmly and in a thoughtful way when asked his opinion about something. Home Daddy yelled at them and made fun of her mother when he didn't like something she said. At church and work, Other Daddy was respected. Home Daddy was avoided. Other Daddy always seemed to make sure no one but the family saw Home Daddy.

"Let it go," she told herself. "There's nothing you can do about it now." Kate had left home soon after graduating from high school, determined to have as little to do with her father as possible. She didn't want his money. She didn't want his affection. She certainly didn't want his apologies. A couple of times lately he'd called her up, in an awkward, halting way, attempting to explain away his more damaging behavior. He had all kinds of excuses for treating all of them that way. She didn't want to hear it. She'd downplayed the negative effects of his behavior in order to withhold the need for a forgiveness she had no intention of bestowing. Now that she thought of it, she should have been like her older sister and just withdrawn completely from the family. If she hadn't shown up for the anniversary party, Other Daddy would have come up with a perfectly plausible reason for her absence.

But her mother had pleaded with her to come—for her sake, for her father's sake. It wasn't worth the bother of explaining why she didn't want to come. She did not want to explain the pain of her childhood to the very person who caused it. She in no way wanted to give him that kind of power over her ever again. So she had downplayed her rage and had shown up for the party, like a good little girl. Playing the part once again.

Leaving the storeroom, she reported back to her sister-in-law about the wine bottles and hurriedly volunteered to take out the trash. "Just like old times," she whispered to herself as she opened the back door, "stuck in the middle of Dad's garbage."

WHAT IS ABUSE?

Many times you have probably asked yourself, *How did my life ever get this way?* I believe that at the core of every eating disorder there lies some sort of abuse or abusive situation—verbal, emotional, physical, or sexual abuse, or a combination of these. When this abuse was added to a family situation where perfectionism and high expectations were the order of the day, your eating disorder became your coping mechanism, your way of masking the real pain in your life.[1]

Who Is Emotionally Abusive?

A person is emotionally abusive who:

1. refuses to consider your opinion and then attempts to force their opinion on you without consideration for your point of view.
2. always has to be right when there is a disagreement.
3. devalues your feelings with phrases like, "You're crazy!" or "How could you think such a thing?"
4. uses unrealistic guilt—guilt that is not in line with the situation—to control your behaviors.
5. commands instead of asks you to do things.
6. brings up past hurts to harm you.
7. verbalizes forgiveness but brings up past issues to prove a point.
8. uses threats, physical force, anger, fear, or intimidation to get one's way.
9. practices conditional love.
10. displays favoritism by comparing siblings.
11. incorporates harsh judgments in their communications, in order to produce feelings of shame.
12. misuses scriptures to get one's way.
13. resorts to screaming, yelling, and name-calling in any context.

Physical and sexual abuse are overt, obvious forms of abuse. They are universally condemned as damaging and harmful. A percentage of those with an eating disorder will have this type of overt abuse as a direct reason for their behavior. For others, however, it can be more difficult to identify what has happened to them as abuse. Sometimes, the seed of an eating disorder may stem from an experience that was not intended as abusive but which produced abusive effects. A thoughtless action or careless phrase can take on a life of its own.

When does a careless phrase become emotional abuse? When does a spanking become physical abuse? When does a loving touch become sexual abuse? As you work to discover your understanding of the truth, these are questions you must ask yourself. If a child is spanked because of the anger of the parent, that spanking is physical abuse. If the touch of a parent is done for sexual gratification, no matter where the child is touched, sexual abuse has occurred.

Proverbs 13:24 says, "He who spares the rod hates his son, but he who loves him is careful to discipline him." Love for the child dictates caution and careful consideration in discipline. As you consider the times when you were physically disciplined by a parent, you will know it as abuse if the discipline was done out of anger and not love.

In the same way, examine how your parents physically interacted with you. Expand that examination to other family members, both immediate and extended. Think about the family relationships you have now. Are they mutually beneficial and uplifting? Or are they one-sided? Consider the following information as you assess your current relationships.

Verbal Abuse

Verbal abuse is one of the most basic and previously overlooked forms of abuse. As a child you were subject to spoken messages from others. These provided the basic structure for your self-identity and self-worth. You trusted those around you to tell you about yourself. If their messages were positive, you learned to love yourself and consider yourself special. But if, from early on, you were told, "You'll never amount to anything!" or "You never do anything right!" or "You were an accident. We never meant to have you," you developed a negative self-image.

Adults tend to underestimate the power of their words to children. Children hear much more than merely the words pointed in their direction. Their "feelers" are constantly on guard, gauging the mood of the adults around them. The caustic word, spoken in the heat of the moment, may affect a child's self-image well into adulthood. In the clarity of an emotionally charged argument, a misspoken word can confirm the natural self-doubt and insecurities of adolescence. The word that twists a child's heart can be spoken in anger or in carelessness. Whispered pronouncements of disgust, disappointment, or disapproval can be as damaging to a child as outward explosions of anger.

Verbal abuse is the consistent pattern of chipping away at the self-image of another person. Think back to the "Food for Thought" section in chapter 3. Look again at the phrases you remember from your childhood. What do these phrases say? Were they positive, uplifting messages, or were they negative messages that caused you to think less of yourself?

Emotional Abuse

Emotional abuse can be either verbal or nonverbal. Teasing, belittling, sarcasm, and taunts are all verbal forms of emotional abuse. Nonverbal abuse might take the form of expecting more from children than they can reasonably deliver. Conditional love, with its message of "I love you, but..." is also a form of emotional abuse.

Emotional and verbal abuse are easy to deny because the scars are hidden; there are no bruises to heal, no visible wounds to point to. It is harder to say, "Yes, this really happened!" If you have always lived with them, these behaviors might even seem "normal" to you. But for all of their seeming invisibility, they can be very damaging.

Physical Abuse

The outward effects of physical abuse are usually easy to see. Not so easy to see are the scars brought about by the constant fear of being hurt, the ever-present threat of physical violence. The fear of physical abuse hangs over a child all the time, never dissipating. The uncertainty of when the next blow will strike is often dreaded more than the blow itself.

Sexual Abuse

These forms of abuse—verbal, emotional, and physical—can be combined with one of the most insidious forms of all, sexual abuse. Sexual abuse need not be confined to intercourse. Best defined as the exploitation of one person for the sexual gratification of another, it can take the form of exhibitionism, fondling, inappropriate touching, or an inappropriate relationship between a child and an adult. When someone you love and trust has treated you this way, you may have blocked out the truth of what was happening to you. In adult life, this may lead to an extreme dislike of hugging, intimacy, or any kind of touching. Research suggests that one in three girls and one in eight boys under the age of 18 will be involved in some sort of forced sexual experience with a grown-up.

Sexual abuse has been shown to have a direct effect on the development of an eating disorder. When a child's thoughts about her body are sabotaged by unwanted sexual attention by an adult, they set in motion a distorted self-image. Studies suggest that the particulars of the sexual abuse can be quite varied; that the important aspect related to eating disorders is the fact of the abuse as opposed to any specific set of circumstances.

Abuse and Posttraumatic Stress

According to the National Institute of Mental Health, children who have been abused are more likely to develop posttraumatic stress disorder (PTSD). This stress need not wait until adulthood to manifest itself. Rather, symptoms can occur in children and adolescents. The memories of childhood abuse can also surface in adulthood, triggered by unrelated traumatic events.

One of the symptoms of PTSD is gastrointestinal discomfort or distress. It is intriguing to consider the possibility that this very symptom of PTSD might actually influence or support a decision to use an eating disorder as a coping mechanism. Take, for example, a child caught in the midst of a marital break-up. The child's anguish could manifest itself in gastrointestinal distress, making it literally painful to eat. The child might decide that, while she cannot decide whether or not her parents fight, she can decide whether or not to endure any additional pain by eating. The physical pain of hunger might even be interpreted as better than the unpleasant side effects of eating with an upset stomach.

Or consider a child who is physically abused by a parent. The stress involved with the uncertainty of when the next blow will fall could manifest itself as a gnawing, rumbling digestive tract. The child could interpret this rolling stomach mistakenly as a sign of hunger. He might then determine that the way to settle his stomach, and his other worries, is to eat—and to keep eating as long as his distress continues.

A child who is convinced of her own unworthiness may decide that the severe restriction of all pleasure, including the enjoyment of eating, is a way to buy penance for her imperfection. Digestion becomes linked to self-love and self-acceptance. By denying the body's basic needs, the soul is punished.

THE POWER OF PAIN

Abuse creates its own rules, not only for the abuser but also in the responses of the abused. The specifics of the abuse may be different, but the effects are often similar.

- Emotional uncertainty leads to persistent self-doubt.
- Sense of shame promotes the thought of unworthiness.
- Loss of control fuels an intense need to find control.

- Creation of a "pain pocket"—a concentration of pain that demands a mood-altering response through addictive behavior.
- Perception of dirtiness results in a variety of methods of "emotional cleansing" through purging, exercise, abstinence, laxatives, and cutting behaviors.
- Preoccupation with self produces unresolved pain, robbing a person of the ability to remove focus from themselves and to transfer it to other people, other points of view, other pleasures.

Understanding your past is not about measuring any abuse you suffered to determine whether it is "weighty" enough to justify your eating disorder. Eating disorders are born out of a child's pain. That pain may come as a direct result of deliberate cruelty by another person or as a consequence of the inattention, neglect, and carelessness of those who should have placed your welfare and happiness at the top of their priority list, but didn't. The pain may also have come as a result of a rigid, tight-fisted control of your emerging individuality and sense of self.

Pain is not something that needs to be justified. In order to heal, pain must simply be understood. Your eating disorder may have masked the pain and numbed the torment. But unrecognized or denied pain is still toxic, harming the fragile sense of self. Your eating disorder has promised you a temporary smoke screen to shield you from the truth, but at the heart of this behavior is obsession and addiction. It's time to clear the air and see your eating disorder for what it really is.

FOOD FOR THOUGHT

In your journal, write out answers to the questions here that apply to you.

1. Is it hard for me to remember what life was like for me growing up?

   The time periods or ages that I cannot remember are…

When I do remember things from my childhood, are they happy memories or stressful ones?

2. When my mother called me to come to her, how did I feel?

   At what times did I wish my mother and father wouldn't notice me?

   When I didn't want my mother or father to notice me, I would...

   When my mother was angry, her voice made me feel...

   If I was afraid of my mother when she was angry, it was because I was afraid she would...

   Did my mother hit me?

3. I was afraid of my father being angry with me when I...

   When my father was angry, his voice made me feel...

   When my father was angry with me, he would...

4. Did my father or mother ever tease me so that I got angry at them? If so, when?

   How did my parents treat me when I hurt myself?

   Being hugged by my parents made me feel...

   How did my parents treat me when I disappointed them?

   When did I stop telling my parents I was hurting? When did I become afraid they didn't care whether or not I was in pain?

   Did I decide that I was a "bad" child?

   Do I remember getting angry at my parents for being uncaring to me?

5. When my parents were angry with me, they would show their anger in the following ways:

   I felt guilty as a child when I…

   I remember being hurt by _____ when I…

   When I was being hurt on the outside, on the inside I felt…

   How did I feel on the inside if my mother or father hurt one of my brothers or sisters?

   When I was hurt, I wished it was _____ instead of me. When one of my brothers or sisters was hurt, I wished it was _____ instead of them.

6. How was my privacy respected by my mother while I was growing up?

   How was my privacy respected by my father while I was growing up?

   When my father touched me _____, I felt uncomfortable. When he would say things like _____, I felt uncomfortable.

   Did he ever make me promise to keep something a secret between us?

   Looking back on it now, from a viewpoint I didn't have then, do I think my father abused me in a sexual way? If so, how?

   Did my mother know? My mother tried to protect me by…

   My mother failed to protect me because…

7. Did one of my parents treat me better than the other did? How?

   If so, did the parent who treated me better know I was being mistreated by the other? If so, what did he or she do to protect me?

8. My anger toward the person who abused me has caused me to…

My anger toward the person who failed to protect me has caused me to…

My anger at myself for what happened has caused me to…

I am holding on to the following resentments:

9. Find a comfortable chair or couch. Give yourself comfort. Hug a pillow, or sit with your knees up and hug your knees. Ask a friend or therapist to say each of these statements to you and then have you repeat them aloud, as loud as you want to.

"I am a special person!"

"I should not have been treated the way I was!"

"I am not responsible for what happened to me!"

"I am angry with the person who made me feel this way!"

"That person had no right to make me feel this way!"

"That person is responsible for what I went through!"

"I am not a bad person! I am a person worthy to be loved!"

"If you could not love me, the fault is yours, not mine!"

"I will not be like you!"

"I will be a person who can give love to others!"

Please go online to www.aplaceofhope.com/audio/
emotionalabuse.html for my special message on abuse.

10. Now set up a chair facing you. Imagine in that chair every person who has hurt you in the past. Tell these people what you've just told yourself. Transfer to them the responsibility for the pain you've been through. Lift the responsibility for the abuse from you and place it on them.

To help visualize this transfer of responsibility, go to your closet and get the biggest, heaviest coat you can find. Put it on. Put on several coats. Go back to your chair and repeat these statements. Lift each coat off yourself and put it on the other chair. Say to yourself that you're going to stop bearing the responsibility for your abuse any longer. Give it back now to the person who gave it to you in the past.

Think about how heavy those coats felt. Then think how they would feel to a child, how they would overwhelm that child if he or she were forced to wear them. Now, think about how much lighter you felt when you took each coat off.

IN THE RIGHT DIRECTION

SWEET RELEASE

Now that you've taken those coats off, don't be surprised if you wake up wearing one or more of them tomorrow. You've worn those coats for a long time now. They fit you. They know your curves, your shape, the hunch of your shoulders, the bend of your elbow.

When you first put them on, they didn't fit. But over time you've tailored those coats to correspond to your needs. As you go through your day, you'll find yourself automatically reaching out and putting them on without ever really thinking about it. As soon as you realize you're wearing one again, stop.

Take it off and put it back on the shoulders of those responsible for your pain. They may not want it, but don't accept it back.

On and off, this resumption and then rejection of responsibility will continue for a time. I hope that each time you take off a coat, it'll stay off a little longer—and when it does come back on, you'll discover it sooner. The more frequently your coat, your false sense of responsibility, is lifted from your shoulders, the easier it will be for you to recognize its weight when it tries to settle back down on you. Be aware of the physical signs you experience when you are wearing it.

Instead of reaching for that coat, be deliberate in your response when someone hurts you today. Develop a different way of reacting to emotional hurt. Don't allow the emotional abuse in your past to preprogram you into reacting, into putting back on that coat, when you are hurt in the present. Otherwise, that coat will never be far from you. Instead, think about the following:

- Recognize the offense for what it is. Intentional? A misunderstanding? Listen to what your heart tells you about what is happening.
- Write out what was said. Does it look different on paper? Write out how you felt about what happened. Use these feelings to decide what to do.
- Resist the tendency to defend your position. If you need to confront the person who hurt you, offer only your point of view about the incident.
- Give up the need to be right.
- Apologize for any legitimate wrongs or oversights you may have contributed to the situation.
- Respond, don't react. This requires you to pause long enough to think and evaluate. Waiting may add perspective.
- Build bridges; don't attack or retreat. Conciliatory attitudes are easier to deal with than hostile, defensive ones. Practice maintaining love and acceptance.

- Realize you may be the target of someone's anger without being the source of it. Take responsibility only for your part.
- Create your limits and insist they be respected.
- Realize that someone's hurting you need not take away your happiness. You are in charge of your attitude and response. You can overcome the hurt.

AFFIRMING ACTION

Realize that you are not diminished by the abuse you have suffered. Consider what is said about Jesus in Hebrews 12:2-3: "Let us fix our eyes on Jesus, the author and perfecter of our faith, who for the joy set before him endured the cross, scorning its shame, and sat down at the right hand of the throne of God. Consider him who endured such opposition from sinful men, so that you will not grow weary and lose heart."

Christ suffered terrible abuse at the hands of men, yet he remained pure, patient, and loving. He has set the example for how to respond through his dying words on the cross: "Father, forgive them, for they do not know what they are doing" (Luke 23:34). Christ was not diminished by his suffering; neither should you be.

God's love allows me to heal from the harm of the past. There is freedom from resentment. I claim this freedom and will walk toward my future of hope.

Cynthia's Story

M y name is Cynthia French.
I suffered from anorexia for seven years and bulimia for over thirteen years. Adding it up, more than twenty years of my life were engulfed in the nightmare of eating disorders. I functioned and was somehow able to accomplish a few things, but the essence of my existence revolved around food—either not eating it or devouring it and bingeing and purging. Nothing took precedence over my diseases.

Now that I look back, I realize that anorexia, bulimia, and binge eating (which I did for seven years before I fell into anorexia) were attempts on my part to fill a deep hole inside of me that I had created from a lack of self-love.

I know that every story of recovery is unique, but there are probably similarities that intertwine all of our experiences. I believe that we are born with the birthright to love ourselves. God gives us that blessing because his love is so unconditional and pure. However, we are influenced by those around us and our environment from day one, so it's understandable that we could learn to despise ourselves if we let vicious, unkind, and demeaning words affect the way we think of ourselves. I was a queen at believing the jealous or mean words of others. I slowly let them mold the way I thought about myself.

As is typical with an anorexic, I couldn't view my body properly. I'd look at myself in the mirror and see a distorted view of myself. I had no idea what I really looked like. How did I overcome?

I have learned that I have the power to do anything and achieve any goal.

When my motivations are love-based, anything is possible. If my motivations are fear-based, I'll make weak choices that will lead to self-destructive behaviors. That's the thing: I was afraid of myself for years, so I didn't think I had the power to *not* be. I felt out of control. That was the disease: my fear of myself. My fear.

What I desire to share is that I healed from eating disorders through a realization that God lives inside of me and is a part of me. He is very real, and when I surrender my own stubborn will to be of service to love, all things come together in such a beautifully simple, truly perfect way. Life flows, all needs are met, and life is full of beauty and joy. This may sound trite, but it is absolutely true.

When I healed from eating disorders, I felt the need to reach out to others who were dealing with or potentially heading toward eating disorders. I wanted to share my story, but desired to do so in a way that would be entertaining as well as healing. So I sat down and wrote a novel, entitled *Humanville*. It shares a story of finding hope, healing, and happiness through learning how to listen and trust our inner voice of love and God.

I see a bright future ahead of me as I walk each day with the knowledge of the power of love. I can choose how I perceive every moment of every day, and every person in my life is touched by my perception. I see myself in a healthy light, and I embrace the lessons learned through this enlightenment. Changing my attitude from fear to love is the most amazing experience I've ever had—the most difficult to come to, but the easiest to achieve. Go figure!

I'm grateful to have the opportunity to share my story, and I'm so thankful for all those who helped me come back to a place of health, happiness, and hope. It's possible. That's a promise!

—Cynthia French
author of *Humanville*
www.humanville.com

Five

The Addiction of Choice

The three-day gospel meeting was nearing its Sunday-night crescendo. The guest speaker from Memphis was working his way up to the spiritual culmination of the evening. Loud "amens" could be heard sprinkled throughout the lilting cadence of his preaching. Justine sat in the third pew from the back and nodded her head along with the rest.

Yes, she believed in God.

Yes, she believed in Jesus.

Yes, she believed in the fallen state of humanity.

Yes, she knew that lying was a sin. So was murder.
   And swearing.

Yes, she knew she needed to tithe. And pray. And repent.

No, she would not commit adultery.

No, she would not smoke cigarettes.

No, she would not consume alcohol.

No, she would not cause a brother or sister to stumble.

She would practice submission and humility. She would live a quiet
   and peaceful life, marked by moderation and restraint.

She would not bring reproach upon the church.

She would strive to be perfect like Jesus was perfect.

Amen.

The preacher continued to verbally pound the air just over the heads of the congregation with his scriptural points, each emphasized consonant resounding like a hammer blow on the head of a nail. Each admonition pierced her heart. Justine felt exposed, yet inexplicably giddy in the knowledge of her sinful state, as if caught in the act of something unmentionable, left with no other response but to giggle in shame.

Redemption was the final act of the drama. "Restoration is possible!" the preacher shouted. "Reconciliation is but a thought away!" he reminded the crowd of mostly regular churchgoers. A chorus of "amens" rose in response to his heated rhetoric. The crowd was firmly in his control, and he knew it. Pausing dramatically, he bowed his head and began to pray out loud for all to hear.

Fully convinced of the certainty of divine wrath and fully convicted of her own unworthiness, Justine crept quietly up to the throne of God in prayer, taking comfort in her own smallness, in her own ability to slip under heavenly radar.

The sermon ended with five people coming forward for confession and two adolescents committing their lives to God. All-in-all, a good three days. With a collective sigh, the congregation began to disperse. Foyer doors opened to let people out and let fresh air in. It twirled into the auditorium, carrying tantalizing odors of the potluck furiously prepared in the fellowship hall.

Say what you like, Justine thought to herself, taking in the heady aroma, *there's one thing this church knows how to do, and that's eat!*

THE CHOICE OF ADDICTION

If love and acceptance were dished out sparingly or not at all when you were growing up, is it any wonder you chose food to fill up the real hunger you felt? If every aspect of your life seemed completely out of your control, is it any wonder you chose controlling the only thing you felt you could—your own body?

In the excellent book *Addiction and Grace,* Dr. Gerald May defines addiction this way: "Addiction is any compulsive, habitual behavior that limits the freedom of human action. It is caused by the attachment, or nailing, of desire to specific objects. The word *behavior* is especially important in this definition, for it indicates that *action* is essential to the addiction." The object of desire for a person with an eating disorder is food. For the bulimic or the overeater, it is the consumption of food. For the anorexic, it is the abstention from food. An eating disorder limits the freedom to eat in a normal, healthy way. The question becomes, when was desire nailed to food?

Eating disorders are all about choices. Each eating disorder is a deliberate choice of how to deal with pain. These choices may have started on a subconscious level. But as the eating disorder progressed, the choices became more and more deliberate and at the forefront of your conscious mind. For many reasons, food has become an integral part of the way you cope with life.

Understanding how you came to choose food as a coping mechanism in the past does not necessarily enable you to deal with an eating disorder in the present. For what began as a method of controlling a difficult, painful situation has now evolved into an addiction. In order to understand the power this addiction has over you, it is important to understand how addictions in general function.

A Rose by Any Other Name

Addictions—whether an eating disorder, alcoholism, workaholism, substance abuse, promiscuity, excessive exercising, gambling, pornography, or others—always appear attractive at first. They promise to deliver exactly what we desire. They even seem to deliver on those promises initially. But like a rose, their attractiveness hides thorns.

- They promise freedom but deliver slavery.
- They are progressive. Addictions don't reveal themselves as such in the beginning. They adopt other names like comfort, coping, control, and they progress to addiction, compulsion, chaos.

- They are deceptive. We use an addiction because we believe it will give us something we need; all the while, the addiction robs us every time we use it.
- They steal intimacy. As we become more intimate with the addiction, we withdraw from other people.
- They promote shame. Becoming overwhelmed by addiction leads to self-hatred, guilt, and shame. The longer the addiction, the deeper the bond of shame.
- They produce spiritual isolation. The power of an addiction can cause the sufferer to doubt the power of God.
- They cause physiological changes. Addictions can act on the pleasure centers of the brain, corrupting the natural processes of body endorphins to subvert the body's "natural high" mechanism. They create nutritional deficiencies and hormonal imbalances that hinder our ability to overcome them.
- They lead us to accept fear and anxiety as normal parts of daily life. With eating disorders, the more we eat, the more we fear. And the more we fear, the more we turn to eating disorders and other compulsive behaviors to cope with the fear.

Misery Loves Company

A food-related addiction can also be accompanied by coaddictions. If you are bulimic, you may binge on food for a period of time, then switch to alcohol in order to become so sick that you throw up. If you are an anorexic, you also may have a greater potential for succumbing to alcohol abuse.

Bulimics may be addicted to cigarettes to help moderate their food cravings. One of the most common coaddictions of the bulimic is prescription medications and even over-the-counter drugs such as diuretics and laxatives. These addictions may work in tandem with your bulimia, compounding your addiction to food.

If you are bulimic or anorexic, you may also have a compulsive tendency to exercise, fueled by your fear of becoming fat. Maybe you believe that if you exercise and don't eat, you'll lose that much more weight. When the obsession with which you conduct your eating disorder is transferred to your exercise program, it becomes just another element in your addiction. You may even experience withdrawal symptoms if you are unable to exercise and feel confused, irritable, anxious, depressed, and listless. You may also feel a loss of self-confidence and self-esteem.

Unlike your eating habits, your exercise regimen does not need to be kept secret. There is no shame involved with it, only the admiration of others for your discipline. If you have an eating disorder, be aware that exercise can become a coaddiction. Even though society praises exercise, those with eating disorders need to be careful not to abuse it.

The Safe Sin

For many people, Christians especially, food is a "safe" addiction. Fire and brimstone are rarely used in reference to gluttony, allowing for compulsive overeating to avoid direct pulpit confrontation. Fasting can be espoused as a spiritual virtue, producing false pride in someone who is anorexic. The sinful nature of the flesh is all too well understood by the bulimic who views purging as a way to rid the body of the sin of consumption.

With alcohol, drugs, sex, even material consumption being frowned upon and openly preached against, some Christians will migrate to food as their safe addiction of choice. This is especially true when fellow brothers and sisters in the faith meet regularly to fellowship accompanied by an overabundance of food. Or when the generous hospitality believers are to show to one another takes the form of multiple dishes and third helpings. Meals define Christian fellowship in many circles, even down to the partaking of the Lord's Supper. Is it any wonder food can become the Christian's addiction of choice?

Religion at its best leads people to an understanding of the grace and mercy of God. Religion at its worst browbeats people with the inevitability of their own sin. Perfectionism, rigidity, a lack of self-worth, and a distrust of compassion are all breeding grounds for both religious toxicity and eating disorders. Is it any wonder these can go hand-in-hand?

Addictions and Attention Deficit Disorder

In *The Link Between A.D.D. and Addiction,* author Wendy Richardson draws a parallel between attention deficit disorder (ADD) and the propensity for addictive behavior, including eating disorders. She states, "ADD is frequently accompanied by other conditions and problems. This is especially true in adults. Few people with untreated ADD make it through adulthood without developing other problems, such as substance abuse, eating disorders, anxiety, depression, low self-esteem, or compulsive behaviors."[1] The author goes on to explain ADD as organic or biological in nature, resulting from brain functioning, specifically neurotransmitters.

Much of the work done in treating eating disorders, and addictions in general, has been in the area of behavior modification, while organic causes have been downplayed. It is important to recognize that there are many factors contributing to an eating disorder, both psychological and physiological. The link between these will be explored further in chapters 8 and 10.

Hearing Society's Message Loud and Clear

Even if an eating disorder is reinforced by an organic, internal reason, there are generally plenty of external reasons for choosing an eating disorder to deal with pain. One of the most powerful reasons to chose an eating disorder comes from the way others view us. Others' acceptance is a powerful enticement. Unfortunately, that acceptance is dictated too often by physical appearance. The pressure to fit a societal mold of physical acceptability comes early and comes hard. How many of the following comments have you either thought yourself or heard from others?

- Members of the opposite sex are only interested if you're physically attractive.

- If she could just lose twenty pounds, then she'd be pretty.
- You have such a pretty *face!*
- Do this and you'll lose weight.
- I don't want a girlfriend who weighs more than I do.
- Just stop eating and you'll lose weight.
- If you're fat, nobody wants you.

FOOD FOR THOUGHT

Looking for the Keys to Addiction

1. Imagine your addiction as a deep pit. Using a page of your journal, draw a picture of your pit of addiction. Take your time and put in lots of detail. Draw the top of the pit, the sides, and especially the bottom. Draw what is inside the pit, either through objects or words.

    Where are you in this picture? Are you at the bottom of the pit? Climbing up the sides? At the top, looking in?

2. How does it make me feel to know I have this pit in my life?

    What is my pit like?

    Is the top easy to see, or is it hidden?

    What are the sides of my pit like?

    Is it easy or hard to climb out of my pit?

    What sorts of things are found in the depths of my pit?

3. How much time do I spend each day in my pit?

    My pit is comfortable because…

    I feel safe in my pit because…

4. What else is in my pit besides food?

   How do the other things in my pit interact with food? How do the other things in my pit help me to keep the food in there?

5. When is the first time I remember going down into my pit?

   It didn't seem like a pit back then because...

6. On another page of your journal, draw a series of tools with which to clean out your pit (for example: a broom, a mop, a stick of dynamite, a bucket of tears). What tools have you chosen, and how will they help you clean up the mess?

7. Now that you've cleaned out your pit, where are you going to put those things? If you don't put them somewhere else, they will want to return to your pit. If you could put them somewhere else, where would that be? If you could give them to someone else, who would that be?

8. If you have gone back to your pit, consider how you would complete the following statements.

   I believe the main reason I returned to my pit was...

   When I was slipping back toward my pit, my warning signs were...

   To stay out of my pit today, I believe I must...

   To stay out of my pit this week, I believe I must...

   To stay out of my pit for the next several months, I believe I must...

Remember, if you begin to feel hopeless—perhaps because of your addiction—you need to get professional help to deal with that hopelessness. Knowing your pit is there is the first step toward climbing out!

IN THE RIGHT DIRECTION

FACING YOUR ADDICTION

You may be having ambivalent feelings toward your pit of addiction, especially as you were drawing it. It may not really look like a pit, and perhaps it hasn't always seemed like a pit to you. Instead, it was a haven where pain couldn't touch you. You thought that by going into this secret place you could escape your pain. You know now that your pain was always there; you brought it with you.

As you think about cleaning out your pit and leaving behind your food addiction, be sure to look into all the nooks and crannies. Watch out for any coaddictions that may be hiding there. You may even be shielding one, holding it in reserve as a substitute for your eating disorder.

Don't despair if you fall back into the hole during your journey. As you become a child again, reliving difficult memories, you may even be surprised to see your pit transform itself. It may suddenly appear to be, once again, the wonderful place of escape it was then.

The temptation will be great to fall back into your pit as the child you were then. But you must climb out of it as the adult you are now. Work at trying to stay away from the edge as much as you can. When you fall back in, work at getting out of it again as fast as you can.

AFFIRMING ACTION

Giving up on dreams can be very difficult. We believe our dreams are what keep us going. But an eating disorder is not a dream; it is a delusion. Though powerful, the addiction is not beyond our ability to overcome. The addiction will deceive us into thinking it is more powerful than anything we can do.

We are not powerless to overcome an addiction when we utilize the power of faith. Hebrews 11:1 says, "Now faith is being sure of what we hope for and certain of what we do not see." The Bible tells us that God is more powerful than our addiction when it says, in Luke 1:37, "nothing is impossible with God." Faith in this promise tells us that God is able to empower us to overcome the bondage of an addiction. Our eyes may not see it, but faith asks our hearts to believe it.

There is victory over my addiction. My faith grows each day.

Six

The Detour of Denial

"Angela, do you remember the first time we met?" he asked her.

Angela had been up front with him that first time in his office. "I'm not interested in dredging up my past," she told him. "I'm here to deal with my weight in the present. Just help me learn how to lose this weight, and we'll get along fine."

She'd seen another counselor about a year earlier, but that one had only wanted to talk about her childhood and how she got along with her parents. That counselor had asked her about her relationships and what she remembered about grade school. Angela had begrudgingly answered with small snippets of information, all the time anxious to deal with her real issue: She was trapped in a mound of flesh, imprisoned by her ever-expanding weight. Something needed to be done about it *right now.* Angela had no time or patience to hash over ancient history or dredge up forgotten slights. The weight wasn't going away, and she was tired of it now.

"I stopped seeing her after three sessions," she remembered telling him that day in his office. After about a year of watching her weight creep up, she had decided to try again. But this time, she was determined to be more in control.

"Sure, I remember the first time we met," she finally answered. "I was just so tired of being fat. It was an effort to get up in the morning, to dress, tie my shoes. When I went out with the kids, I was always straining to keep up, huffing and puffing after them. Nothing ever fit right. Not my clothes, not chairs, not cars. I remember feeling panicked, like I was suffocating in all my fat. I couldn't seem to breathe half the time. My husband had basically given up on our relationship. I hated the way I looked, and I hated myself even more when he looked at me, so I just kept finding ways to avoid him. I was sick a lot, always complaining about how bad I felt, how it hurt to move. Oh, yes," she assured him, "I remember."

He nodded. Of all the things they'd worked on over the past months, that was perhaps the thing that pleased him most: Helping her find the strength to remember.

Of course, it hadn't started out that way. They spoke about what was happening in her life at that moment. He built trust by working from the here-and-now. But once trust was established, he slowly began working Angela back into the past she so adamantly wanted to avoid.

Now, after spending months working through that past, he could easily understand why she avoided it. She had hoped to make things right without acknowledging her past; she was learning she could only make things right by accepting it.

SAY IT AIN'T SO

Individuals with an eating disorder are often unaware of the source of their pain. I believe this is God's way of protecting us. In order to survive as children, we block out abusive behavior. But somewhere along the line, the adult must discover the wellspring of pain from the past. Denial is a significant detour in that quest.

There are two kinds of denial. The first is your own denial of what has happened to you. This may take the form of doubting that what you remember ever took place. Because the abuse has been denied, it may take on an unreal quality when remembered, almost as if it happened to someone else. If the abuse is remembered, it is often seen through a prism that "explains" why the abuse wasn't really abuse at all.

Denial enters through self-talk. These are the messages we repeat over and over to ourselves as we try to deal with the pain and the eating disorder. Thoughts of "nobody's home is perfect" or "it could have been worse" or "it wasn't that bad" or "there's nothing I can do about it now" allow you to minimize the damage. "I should be strong enough to deal with this on my own" or "everyone turns to food when they're down" increases frustration at the inability to bring the eating disorder under control. But denial, this minimization of the pain, is merely a coping mechanism to keep the pain at bay. Denial is the ticket that allows you to transform life-altering pain into that limbo state of "not that bad." If it's "not that bad," you believe you can find the strength to go on.

The other form of denial comes from the person or people who hurt you. They may deny that the abuse ever took place or that there was anything wrong with it if it did. He or she may accept that the event or events happened but deny responsibility or minimize the damage. This can happen regardless of the nature of the abuse. Whether the abuse was a single, specific event or a pattern of hurtful behavior carried out over a number of years, this person may refuse to accept the ramifications of his or her actions.

This person may even attempt to make you feel responsible for the abuse itself or responsible for your "version" of the events. They may deny the damage by calling into question your natural response to the damage. It is to his or her benefit if denial goes both ways—their denial of the event and your denial of the damage done. They may resist acknowledging your eating disorder, because acknowledgement means recognizing the abuse or pattern of hurtful behavior behind it. So the responsibility for the abuse itself and the resulting eating disorder could be shoved back at you, increasing the stress surrounding your eating disorder, escalating its progression. As your eating disorder escalates, it becomes easier to focus your attention solely on its progress, diverting your attention from the root cause.

ANGER'S DEEP ROOTS

Your eating disorder has been with you a long time. Because the attachment to your eating disorder was formed during childhood, its roots dig deep into your being. As you seek to remember the pain from your past, you may find that you crave the security of your eating disorder even more. Being aware of this reaction can help you to put into perspective what you are feeling.

If you are anorexic, the denial of your pain has translated into a denial of your physical state. Under that denial is deep anger. You are dealing with this deep anger by turning it inward, toward yourself, and attempting to control it by controlling your body and food.

If you are a compulsive overeater or bulimic, you know that bingeing or bingeing and purging are unhealthy for you, but you are denying why you do these things. Over the years, your eating habits have covered up your emotions so effectively that now it may be very difficult for you to accept those emotions and what is behind them. You may simply find it easier to say, "I'm a bad person," or, "If I could just find the right diet, I'd be fine."

Why would a person deny a behavior that can lead to so much suffering and misery? If the consequences are so damaging, how can someone continue to deny they exist? Denial may be part of your family upbringing. Just as you learned your eating disorder in childhood, so you also may have learned faulty reasoning patterns. Often these patterns are tied into the family. How did your parents respond to you when you disagreed with them? Could feelings and emotions—positive and negative—be expressed in your family?

Anger is often the emotion of choice for parents in families in which eating disorders develop. Anger is expressed in a variety of forms as a response to the majority of life's situations. The parent is not only angry at the child, but angry at the world. Angry at the other cars on the road. Angry at the family pet for getting in the way. Angry at the paperboy for throwing the paper too far from the front porch. Angry at the neighbor for the noise at their backyard barbecue. Angry at the waiter in the restaurant for taking too long. Angry at coworkers for slacking on the job. Angry at a spouse for being underappreciating. Angry at the oven for burning the roast. Just plain angry.

Though the parent can and does express anger freely in this type of family situation, the child soon learns it is unsafe to express his or her own anger, for fear it will trigger an even greater outpouring of anger by the parent. So anger, hurt feelings, and frustration must be locked away inside, expressed only in private, furtive ways.

If this describes your family situation, the stored-up anger you have been denying for years is fueling your need to abuse food. You've been hiding your anger away because there was never a safe place to let it out. Unable to express your rage, you swallowed it, turning to food as an outlet for release. The mantra became: *If I can control food, I can control my anger. If I can control my weight, I can control my anger.* Or, perhaps, *If I just let myself eat and eat, I will feel comforted in my anger.*

ACCEPTANCE VERSUS DENIAL

It is possible to replace your faulty coping mechanism with healthy skills for withstanding the stresses of life. It is possible to feel anger without feeling rage. Through counseling, you can learn to understand and accept your childhood and its pain. If you can weather the storm of finally learning the truth and giving up your ideal image of the "perfect" family, your pain and hurt can become like parts of a puzzle, fitting into place and giving you a greater understanding of why your parents do what they do. Once you understand the why, you can begin the process of filling in the void in your life with healthy choices: with laughter and love, with family and friends, with good things, and with God.

Verbal and/or emotional abuse leaves no visible scars, so the tendency to deny that these events happened can be very great. Often the parent will remember the circumstances from a very different perspective than the child. Your child-self recalls one version of events, and your parent another. Which is right? They may both be. When you were a child, you remembered things from the perspective of a child, often unaware of the larger picture. Your parents may never have considered how their actions looked from the other side. Take that into consideration when examining the past. You will need to accept their version of what happened, and they must accept yours. Finding the truth and working with your family will not be easy, but it can be extremely illuminating and rewarding. It can mean the reconciliation of relationships. Or you can gain an understanding of the type of relationship you can realistically have with your family as an adult. Much will depend upon the hurtful behavior and that person's willingness to accept your pain.

Egregious physical or sexual abuse, by its very nature, may lead to outright denial by the abuser. The more valid the memory, the more vehement the denial. Because societal and religious condemnation of such acts is so great, the person who abused you may never truly admit what he or she has done. The abuser may believe that if the abuse is denied outright, you may begin to doubt that it occurred at all. In spite of this, you need to realize that you were hurt. Sometimes it really doesn't matter if memories are totally clear or recalled; you still felt hurt.

The next point is so important, I want to put it in bold type to make sure you don't overlook it.

Your self-destructive behavior did not come about for no reason. Most people who develop a severe eating disorder have had some history of abuse, and I encourage you to believe in what your past reveals. You must be determined to examine your past and accept the truth that is revealed. You must take the truth of your past and put it into perspective as an adult.

Don't allow denial, your own or others, to halt your journey toward healing and recovery.

FAMILY IQ TEST

Dr. Jim Burns, in his book *How to Be a Happy, Healthy Family,* highlights fifteen traits that make for healthy families and comes up with an insightful

"Family IQ (Intimacy Quotient) Test." You can use this test in a couple of different ways. If you are currently still living in the family of your childhood or have yet to establish a separate family of your own, answer these questions as they relate to your parents, as opposed to a spouse, and to your family situation as a whole.

If you currently are in your own family and have left the family of your childhood, take this test first as it relates to the family of your childhood. Put yourself back in the position of a child growing up in that family. Then, take the test again, this time as it relates to the family you are part of now. Do these together so that you can compare how the family of your childhood may intersect your current family dynamic.

Rate Your Family IQ (Intimacy Quotient)

How close is your family? In Dr. Burns's book, Dolores Curran (author of *Traits of a Healthy Family*, Ballantine, 1983) evaluates fifteen traits that go together to make healthy families. The following questions are adapted from her research.

How to Take This Test

Rate the intimacy quotient of your family by responding to the questions. Award yourself points for each answer as follows:

> 1 point: We're definitely not there yet.
>
> 2 points: This is sometimes true of our family.
>
> 3 points: This is usually true of our family.

Then add up your points. (There are two questions representing each trait—in random order.)

> If your total score is 1-30: Your family has the potential to become an intimate family if you are willing to apply energy and determination to the process.

30-60: Your family has a strong foundation upon which to build further intimacy.

60-90: You are maintaining strong momentum in the direction of intimacy.

🍎 🍎 🍎

In our marriage, my spouse and I share power equally, complementing each other's strengths and weaknesses.

At the dinner table, our family shares more than food. We also share ideas, feelings, disappointments, and dreams.

If there is a conflict between a family tradition and an outside responsibility, the family tradition usually wins.

As parents, we allow our children freedom to make decisions in certain areas and expect them to accept the consequences of those decisions.

Our family shares together in at least one leisure activity a week.

As parents, we are aware of our children's facial expressions, body language, and physical gestures and from these pick up clues that lead us to ask appropriate questions and initiate honest discussion.

The basic, underlying mood of our family is hopeful and forward-looking; we have our sources of stress, but we consider them temporary and manageable.

When we are alone together, my spouse and I are vulnerable to each other and risk exposure of our deepest feelings.

We allow our children to make choices between various activities outside the family, but we do not allow these activities to interfere routinely with our leisure time together.

We have different rules for children of different ages.

We know what we believe, and we find strength in our faith.

We have a vision as a family and seek to be involved in something bigger than the quality of our relationships.

We have our share of problems, but we usually can see the positive in every situation, no matter how bad.

No matter how busy we are, our entire family eats a meal together at least once a day.

My spouse and I agree on what is right and wrong.

We make an effort to gather regularly with those in our extended family.

We refuse to remove obstacles from our children's lives that will potentially foster their growth and responsibility.

As parents, we occasionally spend time alone with each of our children.

We keep our work commitments under control and do not allow them to routinely crowd our family.

Although we go through rough periods, we stick together and try to make things right.

In our family, we make each other feel important by supporting each other in our failures as well as in our successes.

As parents, we allow our children to be exposed to situations in which they can gradually earn more trust or rebuild trust-worthiness.

When conflicts arise, we give everyone a chance to speak and work at negotiating solutions before the conflicts become volatile.

Different personality styles and preferences are accepted within our family life.

Our definition of success is not based on promotions, possessions, or power, but in the quality of our service to others.

We laugh at ourselves and with each other, and we use humor to defuse potentially stressful situations.

As adults, we provide for our kids a value system out of which certain rules and accepted behaviors arise.

We present opportunities in our home for our children to prove their capabilities.

The underlying religious attitude of our family is one of moving closer to a shared core of spirituality.

We expect and allow our children to change as they move from age to age. We respect their fads, friends, confidences, privacy, and time—their right to be alone and their right to be different—as long as these things are not destructive.[1]

Looking at the dynamics of your past and/or present family will help you move beyond denial to truth. Loosening the bonds of denial will undoubtedly uncover unpleasant memories and emotions, but it will also begin to free you from the bonds of your eating disorder.

FOOD FOR THOUGHT

Dealing with Emotions from the Past

1. When I was growing up, my mother would release her anger by…

   When my father was really angry, he would…

   When I get angry today, I deal with it by…

2. When I would disagree with my mother, she would…

   When I would disagree with my father, he would…

   I stopped disagreeing with my parents because they never…

3. I remember one time my mother got really mad because I…

   I remember one time my father got really mad because I…

4. In my family, you didn't show you were angry. You also didn't show you were _____ because…

I feel angry now when I remember…

The following things make me really angry:

I have a hard time telling people I'm angry with them because I think they will…

5. When I think back to when I was hurt by _____, I feel _____ because…

When I think back to that time, I wish I could…

6. As you read the following story, put yourself in Rebecca's place.

Rebecca was so excited because Mommy *finally* agreed she could help bake cookies. Rebecca loved cookies, and today they were going to make chocolate chip, her favorite. After they mixed the dough, Rebecca scooped it in little dollops onto the cookie sheet. The smell of cookies baking soon filled the kitchen, and Rebecca's stomach began to rumble in anticipation.

"Can I take the first batch out of the oven, Mommy?" Rebecca asked hopefully.

"No," her mother replied, "they'll be too hot."

"Please!" Rebecca pleaded. "I'll be careful. I promise."

"Well, all right. But make sure you use an oven mitt."

"Oh, I will." Rebecca went to the drawer and brought out a large green mitt, the one that Mommy always used when she took things out of the oven.

Two things happened at once: The timer for the cookies went off, and the telephone rang in the next room.

"Be careful with the cookies!" Rebecca's mother called out as she ran to get the phone.

A blast of heat hit Rebecca in the face as she opened the oven. Wiggling her hand deeper into the mitt, she grasped hold of the hot cookie sheet and extracted it ever so carefully from the oven.

She had just cleared the oven door when she glanced up and realized she hadn't cleared off a space on the counter for the cookie sheet.

Frantically she looked left and right, trying to find somewhere, *anywhere,* to put the cookie pan. Heat was seeping rapidly through the green mitt. Rebecca tried to shift the pan in her grasp so her fingers wouldn't feel like they were burning off.

As she was trying to move her fingers inside the mitt, she lost hold of the cookie sheet. It slipped and fell with a loud *clang* to the floor.

As I read this story, I felt...

Here is what I think happened next:

If I had been Rebecca and that had been my mother, this story would have happened differently because...

7. Now go back and reread the story, only this time put yourself in the place of the mother.

If I had been Rebecca's mother, I would have...

When Rebecca dropped the cookie sheet, I would have...

In what ways are my reactions different from what my mother's would have been? In what ways are they the same?

Whose fault is it that the cookie sheet ended up on the floor? Why?

8. Go back and rewrite the story. Change whatever details you like to make it just the way you'd want it to read. Think about what you're feeling as you go back and "make everything all right."

IN THE RIGHT DIRECTION

DEALING WITH DENIAL

The desire to go back and rewrite your past is seductive, especially if your past was one of abuse and pain. Denial allows you to do just that. Denial takes the pages of your past and alters them according to "if onlys," or it substitutes blank pages for the pain that's really there.

A familiar proverb assures us that those who refuse to learn the lessons of history are doomed to repeat them. It can also be said that those who deny the events of their own history are doomed to relive them. To deny abuse is to perpetuate it. The only way to stop the chain of abuse from your parents, to yourself, to others through you is to stop denying the truth of that abuse.

Each of us is the product of our experiences, and not one of us is immune to the pain they have caused us. We may not be able to control what happened to us, but we can control who we become as a result of those past events.

First, however, you need to look at those experiences honestly. The light of reality can seem harsh and bright to one who has been hiding from the truth, but colors you've never seen await you. Clarity and detail spring forth from the light of truth. The tears you shed on your journey are your eyes watering as they adjust to the light.

AFFIRMING ACTION

Truth can be harsh. The truth of our sin is as harsh as a man dying on a cross. But the truth of Christ does not end with the crucifixion. After the crucifixion comes resurrection. As you put to death your denial, you resurrect truth. As you resurrect truth, you loosen the power your eating disorder has over you. This will not be an easy thing to do, but you have as your ally one who spent three days in the grave himself to be raised to a new life. Please, do not lose hope. Please, do not give up.

God gives me courage each day as I walk out my healing journey.

Seven

When Pain Turns to Pride

"Amber, you've got to start eating. This dieting of yours is going too far."

How many times have I heard that, Amber thought. Instead of responding to her father's comment, she just kept her face turned away from him, concentrating on the scenery flashing by the car window. *Just don't say anything and he'll stop. Even if he doesn't, we'll be at school in a few more minutes.*

"Your mother and I have talked, and both of us agree you're becoming too thin. It isn't healthy."

Just don't say anything.

Inside, of course, Amber had plenty to say to her father. *Since when did you start caring about what's healthy? You never get out and exercise, you never care what you eat, you smoke, you sit around all day long at work—who are you to start lecturing me about what's healthy? And when did you start caring about how much I eat? You're not home for dinner half the time, anyway. If I put on weight, I'm chubby. If I diet, I'm too thin. There's never any pleasing you!*

By this time, Amber was screaming at him inside. On the outside, she affected a disinterested, vacant look, with her arms wrapped securely around her middle and her thighs pressed tightly together. She was physically closing herself off to him, as she inwardly raged at his comments.

"If this goes on too much longer, steps will have to be taken."

Here it comes: the threat. You and mom are so good at the threat. "If you don't clean up this room, you're not spending the night at Sarah's!" "If you talk back like that to me one more time, I'll wash your mouth out with soap, young lady!"

"If you don't start doing better in school, you won't be allowed to continue with dance classes!" "If you don't start getting to bed on time, you'll be on curfew for a week!" "If this goes on too much longer, steps will have to be taken!"

Yeah, like what steps? she asked him silently, lips clenched in a thin, unhappy line. *Are you going to start forcing food down my throat? Like you force me to do everything else I don't want to do? It's my body, and I'll eat what and when I want. You, with your middle-age paunch, what do you know about "too thin"? What do you know about my life? I have to be thin in order to dance. I have to be thin to get dates. I have to be thin to be popular. I have to be thin, period. You're just mad that there's something about me you can't control. Mom's just mad that I'm thinner than she is. If you want to harp on somebody about their weight, harp on her. She's the one with a weight problem.*

At that, the car pulled up to the high school. Without looking at him or saying a word, Amber opened the door and climbed out of the car.

"We are not through with this discussion, Amber," her father warned her as she started to close the car door. She wanted to slam it shut, to yell at him to shut up, but she controlled herself and closed it with a soft push. Gathering up her composure and her books, she walked toward the school entrance.

It may not be over for you, but it is for me. I'm fine. I'll be as thin as I want to be.

FROM DENIAL TO PRIDE

One of the prime factors in denial of an eating disorder is pride. An eating disorder begins as a way to cope with pain, but along the way pride can take root. In the beginning, pride at your cleverness in handling the pain through the eating disorder motivates you. Along the way, pride keeps you blind to the fact that your behavior is abnormal. And in the end, pride hinders you from admitting you have a problem and getting the help you need to recover. All along the way, you must deal with pride.

It feels good to be able to get a handle on a weight problem, to be able to keep your weight down and still eat the things you like. If feels good to be able to exhibit the strength to deny yourself what those around you cannot. It makes you feel good and powerful. Pride tells you, "I can get away with this." It tells you, "I can manipulate this for my own gain." Pride says, "I can get my needs met this way." It promises, "I can do this myself."

As with any addiction, what makes you feel good in the beginning soon ends up controlling your behavior. Then you don't feel so good anymore. But what do you do when the good feelings stop? Pretend your addiction really isn't so bad? Believe you can stop any time you want?

Pride sets up a pattern of self-absorption and leads to an exaggerated

The Cost of Denial and Pride

Maintaining the illusion of the false reality requires:

- self-absorption and self-attention, producing greater amounts of isolation.
- ignoring physical pain and healthy body needs.
- hiding the truth from self and others and constructing an elaborate rationale system.
- maintaining the belief of being better than others, above others, beyond others.
- adhering strictly to perfectionistic thinking and oppressive demands on self.
- an overwhelming attention to food, leaving no time or energy to focus on the ultimate source of the pain.
- total allegiance, turning friends into enemies and loved ones into betrayers.
- abandoning the truth and forfeiting joy and peace.
- denying your true, gifted self.
- more than you are able to give.

sense of self-importance. The negative circumstances that feed into an eating disorder are internalized and regurgitated as a positive display of personal power and accomplishment. Not only is there pride in surviving the pain, but there is tremendous pride in turning that pain around and using it for personal gain. The pain then is perceived as ultimately positive. The anger produced by the pain is relished for its role in strengthening the resolve to continue the eating disorder.

This leads to a created reality where pain is positive, anger is empowering, food is compensation, thin is vindication for the anorexic or bulimic, and fat is defiance for the compulsive overeater. Pride flourishes within this false reality. Every comment, every situation, every relationship is filtered through this false reality. Anything that doesn't measure up or is in contrast to this carefully constructed reality is rejected. Concern over your behavior is scorned, distrusted, rejected. Negative consequences are embraced instead of feared. Warnings are ignored or denied.

If you are anorexic, you've got denial and pride down pat—and you take an enormous amount of pride in the accomplishment of your weight loss. If you overeat, you may tell yourself that your behavior is normal due to your difficult circumstances—*I just need to feel better and then I'll stop.* If you are a compulsive overeater, you are probably past the point of pretending that what you do is normal, but your pride may be keeping you from crying out for help. You may prefer to keep your disorder as your "best friend." You may even have picked up this book with that thought in mind.

The pride that keeps you immobile, unable to break its hold and admit you need help, is a learned response. Some families display a patterned, prideful response based on presenting a "perfect face"—to each other and to the rest of the world. Since you learned your pride from your family, you should not be surprised if that prideful pattern affects your family's ability to see your disorder or to admit their role in its creation.

If you live with or spend time with a person who has a faulty pattern of pride, eventually you will be hurt. Prideful people will use all sorts of ways to build themselves up at your expense: put-downs, shame, belittling, sarcasm. If a family member treated you this way, it is likely that you learned a faulty pattern of pride and that it helped you learn or continue your eating disorder. People with eating disorders are inappropriately concerned with themselves. How you look and what you weigh are your major concerns. Not being fat and ugly is your obsessive goal. But look again: Your goals and concerns are completely self-directed. Pride has been used as an insulator to ward off pain, anger, and shame.

The excessive pride of others caused your eating disorder in childhood. Your excessive pride in adulthood is contributing to your disorder by promoting denial. You must not let this pride become a trap that you cannot climb out of as an adult. You need to admit how much time and energy you devote to thinking exclusively about your body and how you look.

All people have times in their lives when they must focus almost exclusively on themselves in order to survive. For you, these crises occur on a regular basis, both as a result of your disorder and because you manufacture these crises as an excuse for your disorder. For example, an innocuous comment about how you look might throw you into a crisis of starvation or binge-purge, sure that the comment had some deep critical meaning. A glance in a store window may throw you into such despair you drown your frustration over your weight in enormous amounts of food, sure that comfort is worth the cost.

Central to healing is being able to focus outside of yourself, to reduce your level of self-absorption. Being able to look at others as allies instead of competitors is vital in grasping reality. Not only do these attitudes allow you to see the world as it really is—and yourself as others see you—but they help you to find other people who can interact with you, providing you with the support you need on your journey.

When you finally do climb up out of the trap of pride, you may want to go back to your family to try to resolve past conflicts. Your family, which may still be stuck in their own pride, may not want to admit the pain you've been through. Perhaps by understanding how pride has played a part in your own life, you will be better able to understand the role it is playing in theirs.

FOOD FOR THOUGHT

A Good, Hard Look at Pride

Read over the following list of characteristics of a prideful person. This isn't about taking healthy pleasure in one's accomplishments. The following are the characteristics of people whose actions and relationships are driven by pride.

At the end of each characteristic, there is space for you to write about how it applies to someone from your past and how it might apply to you. Remember to be honest with yourself. Your pride will attempt to keep you from answering these questions as openly as you should.

A prideful person:

1. *Won't admit error.* When confronted with an error, the prideful person will attempt to explain it away. She does not want to admit responsibility.

    How this applies to _____:

    How this applies to me:

2. *Needs to win when dealing with others.* She is highly competitive in tasks and relationships.

    Times when I see this characteristic in _____:

    Times when I see this characteristic in myself:

3. *Takes inappropriate authority over other people, even if the authority is not rightly hers.* A prideful person attempts to control circumstances by forcing authority and decisions on to others.

I've allowed _____ to do this to me in the past when she...

I've done this to _____ in the past when I...

4. *Has a tendency to shame others.* In an attempt to build up herself, a prideful person will press down others through shame and humiliation.

   How this applies to _____:

   How this applies to me:

5. *Overuses sarcasm.* The sarcasm need not be directed at you, but may be about other people, places, or things. The overuse of sarcasm gives the impression that the prideful person has some sort of "inside knowledge" not available to others.

   When someone around me is being sarcastic, it makes me feel...

   When I am being sarcastic with others, I feel...

6. *Takes things to extremes.* A prideful person often resorts to excesses when dealing with tasks or other people. She has an exaggerated sense of self-importance.

   I take the following things, besides food, to extremes:

   When I realize that these things are so important to me, it makes me feel...

7. *Has difficulty developing intimacy.* A prideful person often confuses sex with love.

   When I'm with _____, I feel like sex and love are being confused because...

   The differences between sex and love are:

8. *Denies events or characteristics that don't fit her own self-image.* Denial of these is usually accomplished with hostility.

   The person I know who most closely fits that description is _____, because...

   I deny the following things to keep up my self-image of being _____:

9. *Takes pleasure in the distress of others.* Seeing others brought down by suffering or troubles elevates the prideful person.

   How this applies to _____:

   How this applies to me:

10. *Feels a need to be in control of people and circumstances.* The prideful person manipulates events and people to show self in the best possible light.

    The first time I remember being manipulated by someone else was when I was...

    I gain control of others by...

11. *Is critical of self and others.* A prideful person practices and expects perfection.

    _____ expected me to be perfect in the following ways:

    Why I think it's wrong not to be perfect:

12. *Won't receive the criticism of others.* Since the prideful person is so self-critical, she claims to be the only one qualified to judge, chastising herself for an error yet denying it if it's pointed out by someone else.

How this applies to _____:

How this applies to me:

13. *Is really compensating for intense feelings of insecurity.* The prideful person, who uses perfection as the standard of performance, is constantly disappointed in self and others. This results in feelings of guilt and failure, which require even more rigid diligence to combat, resulting in a vicious cycle of shattered expectations.

    I shattered _____'s expectations by not…

    My own perfectionism is covering up the following feelings of insecurity:

14. *Punishes others when they don't act "correctly."* Prideful people project their own judgment of self onto others.

    I've seen _____ portray this characteristic toward _____, and it made me feel…

    Areas where I project my own behavior onto others:

15. *Places blame for failure onto others.* Prideful people will go to great lengths to convince themselves and others that their own errors are actually the responsibility of someone, or something, else.

    _____ has always blamed me for…

    One failure in my life I want to blame on other people is…

16. *Has a self-righteous attitude.* Since prideful people spend so much time elevating themselves by putting down others, they develop a superior-inferior attitude toward the people around them.

    How this applies to _____:

How this applies to me:

Think about your relationship with the other person(s) you've listed. How has that relationship affected how you relate to yourself and others today?

As you were going through this list, was it easier to see the pride in others or in yourself? Why do you think that is?

IN THE RIGHT DIRECTION

FACING YOURSELF

A part of you may be telling yourself that even working on this book is a self-absorbed activity. In a way, you're right. This book requires you to spend an enormous amount of time thinking about who you are. But really looking at yourself honestly is not self-absorption; it is introspection. Self-absorption leads to a false reality; introspection leads to insight. Insight leads to truth.

We all have times in our lives when we need to concentrate on ourselves in order to survive. This is definitely one of those times for you. Your eating disorder has brought you to a point where you're seeing that this book is really addressing your *survival.*

Pride—both your own and that of those who hurt you—will work against your recovery. Faulty pride cannot coexist with perceived imperfection; it's impossible to be prideful when you recognize your own flaws and weaknesses so clearly. You're beginning to understand that your eating disorder was not the "perfect" solution it promised to be. You're starting to remember that yours wasn't the "perfect" family after all. You're now seeing that your pursuit of being "perfect" yourself isn't bringing you any sense of peace.

It's all right to admit that you've made mistakes. To do so is simply to recognize your humanity. And it's perfectly fine to recognize the mistakes of others; you're simply seeing them for who they really are. It's okay to understand the way others' mistakes have affected you; you're simply accepting reality.

Accepting reality means facing the pain and discomfort in order to process it and place it in its proper context. Within that context, your pain will cease to wield such unhealthy power over you. The truth will weaken the hold your self-destructive behaviors have over you. Truth is not something to fear; rather, it is something to be embraced. The truth will not diminish you, no matter how much your false reality says it will. The truth will complete you, giving you needed understanding of yourself and others. The truth will enable you to operate from a new reference point of strength so you can deal with future hurts, pain, and frustration.

AFFIRMING ACTION

False realities do not dissipate quickly. They are stubborn and hold on for dear life. But you must let them go. If you don't, you won't be able to change from wanting to die to wanting to live. You must let go of pride.

Coming out of the darkness of a false reality of pride is not an overnight trip. It will require determination, perseverance, and faith. It will require an acceptance of your own weakness and an admission of your own need for God to strengthen you. The false pride of perfectionistic thinking will war against doing this. It will tell you that you need to be better or farther along in your journey before you can ask God for anything. It will whisper to you that God will not help you.

Do not listen! Listen instead to God himself, in Isaiah 41:10: "So do not fear, for I am with you; do not be dismayed, for I am your God. I will strengthen you and help you; I will uphold you with my righteous right hand."

This promise is your reality.

I have courage. With God's healing grace, I am moving from self-absorption to self-acceptance.

Eight

Making Your Body Your Friend

Maneuvering through the holiday rush of shoppers, Christina felt like a salmon struggling upstream. *Why is it that everyone in the world seems to be walking the other way?* It was exhausting, and besides, she was cold. Her feet hurt, she was jostled left and right by the human torrent, and she was just plain tired. *What are all these people still doing out at 8:45 at night?*

Up ahead lay the doorway to a small jewelry shop. A "closed" sign in the window made it seem out-of-place amid the open storefronts awash in blazing lights, hawking for seasonal shoppers. With great relief, Christina darted out of the flow and rested for a moment in front of the closed door. In the single bulb over the doorway, she could see her reflection in the darkened window. Transfixed, she leaned toward the glass, gazing intently at her own face.

God, I've aged.

Under the harsh light in the doorway, beyond the sea of people, Christina looked at herself in solitude. Her hair was thin and lifeless. Her face, dry and flaccid. Her eyes, dull and rimmed with red.

Under the thick fabric of her coat, the skin on her upper arms drooped, robbed of muscle tone. Her body was an odd mix of thin limbs and stubborn stores of fat, seemingly as double-minded about itself as she was.

The whole thing had started as a way to improve her looks. All it had done over the years was wear her body down. She was tired all the time. Tired of the constant battle with her body. At some point, her body had ceased to be her subservient ally and become an active enemy. She'd stopped purging several years ago, after her teeth got bad from all of the vomiting. Everything was supposed to be fine after she stopped purging.

But the desire to binge continued, even after the purging stopped. She remembered how clever she felt when she decided to go from bingeing and purging to bingeing and starving. The bingeing fed her craving for sweets and comfort food; the starving fed her craving for self-punishment and deprivation.

The great idea hadn't delivered, however. When she binged, she felt bloated; when she starved, she felt sucked dry. There was never any happy medium. There was never any happy *anything*. Trapped in that silent eddy, Christina felt like weeping.

I want my life back, she thought. *I want my health back. I want my strength back. I want to be happy again.*

NATURAL CONSEQUENCES

I believe that physical health is the most overlooked area in the treatment of eating disorders. Because of the physical strain your food addiction has put on your body, you may be fighting not only your denial of the past but also your own body as you attempt to recover. It is vital for you to address the physical—as well as the emotional—ramifications.

Just as it takes time and attention to deal with your emotional health, it will take time and attention to deal with your physical health. It may seem that working on two fronts is more than you are able to do, but the physical and emotional go hand-in-hand. Paying attention to one will benefit the other.

Yeast Infections

There are several common conditions that plague people with eating disorders. The first is a yeast infection known as *Candida albicans*. Symptoms of candida include depression, suicidal urges, loss of sex drive, constipation, diarrhea, and acne. Candida thrives in the warm places of the body: the intestinal tract, the anus, the nose and throat, and the vagina. Around 90 percent of the people I treat for eating disorders suffer from this yeast infection.

When you abuse your body by starvation or through the binge-purge cycle, you upset the natural balance of healthy bacteria that are your body's best line of defense against candida. And since candida thrives on sugar, it can make your physical cravings for food, especially sweets and carbohydrates, extremely intense.

Candida has been overlooked in the past because it can mimic a number of other conditions, such as allergies, infections, and even multiple sclerosis. Unexplained constant pain in the body, especially in the digestive system, can be a result of candida. Often antibiotics are prescribed to fight the infection. But antibiotics have been shown to lower the body's natural defense system, suppressing its ability to produce the healthy bacteria in the intestinal tract that can combat candida. This accounts for the phenomenon of taking an antibiotic for an unrelated problem and experiencing a yeast infection shortly after. Birth control pills may also contribute to candida.

My experience has taught me that people with eating disorders who are

---

An additional source of good information about candida is *The Yeast Connection* by Dr. William G. Crook. The following questionnaire, adapted from Dr. Crook's book, is a quick way to identify whether health problems are yeast connected:

1. Have you taken repeated "rounds" of antibiotic drugs?
2. Have you been troubled by premenstrual tension, abdominal pain, menstrual problems, vaginitis, prostatitis, or loss of sexual interest?
3. Does exposure to tobacco, perfume, and other chemical odors provoke moderate to severe symptoms?
4. Do you crave sugar, breads, or alcoholic beverages?
5. Are you bothered by recurrent digestive symptoms?
6. Are you bothered by fatigue, depression, poor memory, or "nerves"?

treated for candida have an increased rate of physical and emotional recovery. Once their physical condition is improved, they find the strength and greater emotional endurance for a complete recovery on every level.

Currently, one of the most common treatments of candida is a drug called Nystatin, which is itself derived from bacteria. I have found, however, that this drug is not always an effective treatment for those with eating disorders and that many complain of depression and other side effects after taking it.

In my treatment of candida, I've used a special formula called *Canditrol,* an effective yeast killer that contains potassium sorbate.[1] Most people need to take this formula for two to three months. I also advise the elimination of as much sugar and refined carbohydrates from your diet as possible.

Acidophilus is another important dietary supplement. Many dairy products are available with acidophilus, from yogurt to milk. I recommend an acidophilus formula called *Ultra Flora Plus* to aid in digestion and to help balance the levels of beneficial intestinal bacteria.

---

7. Are you bothered by hives, psoriasis, or other chronic skin rashes?

8. Have you ever taken birth control pills?

9. Are you bothered by headaches, muscle and joint pains, or feeling uncoordinated?

10. Do you feel bad all over—without any specific, diagnosed cause?

- If you answer yes to 3 or 4 questions, yeasts *possibly* play a role in causing your symptoms.
- If you answer yes to 5 or 6 questions, yeasts *probably* play a role in causing your symptoms.
- If you answer yes to 7 or more questions, yeasts *almost certainly* play a role in causing your symptoms.[2]

Hypoglycemia

Along with candida, prolonged eating disorders can result in hypoglycemia, which is the body's inability to properly regulate blood sugar. This is especially true of bulimia, with its binge-purge cycle. The inability to properly regulate blood sugar results in large and rapid swings in blood sugar levels. When blood sugar levels drop off drastically, the binge urge can be triggered. Failure to address hypoglycemia can lead to diabetes later in life.

If you suffer from any of the following symptoms, you may have hypoglycemia:

- extreme shifts in energy levels
- mood swings (particularly depression)
- not feeling "good" until you get a fix of some high-calorie food
- a craving for sweets
- problems with equilibrium
- blurred vision
- feeling tired all the time
- hungry between meals or at night
- difficulty sleeping
- increased anxiety levels
- difficulty concentrating or making decisions

For more information, I suggest reading the section on hypoglycemia in Maureen Kennedy Salaman's book *All Your Health Questions Answered Naturally.* When hypoglycemia is treated, candida, if present, can also be greatly reduced. These two conditions often go hand-in-hand, although they may not necessarily coexist.

Food Sensitivities

Prolonged eating disorders can also lead to food sensitivities and the digestive disturbances that lead to food sensitivities. For example, eating "safe" food exclusively—such as carrots—overloads the body and can lead to digestive problems. In addition, over time, food sensitivities can lead to food allergies. Some of the symptoms of food allergies come about after candida has been present; all of these conditions tend to feed on and aggravate each other. Food allergies cause a great strain on our immune system.

The symptoms of food sensitivities are very closely related to those of hypoglycemia:

- depression
- drowsiness
- fatigue
- learning disorders
- anxiety
- insomnia
- hyperactivity
- poor memory and concentration
- personality changes
- social isolation and withdrawal
- angry outbursts
- hallucinations
- delusions
- dizziness
- hot flashes
- confusion
- headaches
- seizures

Food allergies can also affect your respiratory system and lead to difficulty in breathing, asthma, wheezing, coughing, and hyperventilation.

Bedwetting has also been linked to food allergies, along with an urgent need to urinate, painful urination, or the need to urinate several times during the night. For women, food allergies can cause irregular or painful periods and an increase or decrease in sexual drive.

A physician or nutritionist should be able to give you more information on food sensitivities and allergies. Each individual should receive a personalized analysis to determine how to best integrate nutritional support into long-term recovery from an eating disorder. A component of the whole-person care given to those I am treating for an eating disorder includes such a personalized analysis as a basis for long-term, step-by-step physical and nutritional recovery.

If you discover that you have a sensitivity or allergy to a particular food,

Physical Problems Brought On by Eating Disorders

Gastrointestinal

External Problems: Constipation, hemorrhoids

Internal Problems: Insufficient material and fluid

Cause: Failure to take in or retain sufficient food and fluid

External Problems: Swelling and puffiness, especially
    in the ankles and feet

Internal Problems: Electrolyte imbalance, general system problems

Cause: Malnutrition, frequent vomiting, excessive laxative
    or diuretic use

External Problems: Swelling over stomach or abdominal area

Internal Problems: General system problems

Cause: Long periods of starvation, excessive vomiting, excessive
    laxative or diuretic use

Sexual

External Problem: No menstrual period

Internal Problem: Inability to produce hormones

don't allow yourself to become overly distressed. You will be able to find many substitutes, and whatever the disadvantages of no longer being able to consume a particular food, they are far outweighed by the freedom from serious, debilitating side effects.

Premenstrual Syndrome

If you are female, another factor that could be affecting your body is premenstrual syndrome (PMS). PMS is a catch-all phrase for the variety of

Cause: Lack of body fat, rigorous exercise, emotional
   distress, bingeing and purging

Salivary Glands

External Problems: Swelling, pain,
   tenderness

Internal Problem: Possible infection

Cause: Frequent vomiting

Teeth

External Problems: Frequent cavities

Internal Problems: Erosion of tooth enamel

Cause: Inadequate diet, frequent vomiting, high intake
   of carbohydrates/sugars

Skin

External Problems: Dryness, fine rash, pimples

Internal Problem: Dehydration

Cause: Reduced fluid intake, excessive fluid elimination,
   frequent vomiting, laxative abuse

symptoms resulting from hormonal fluctuations, primarily estrogen and progesterone. With PMS, there is a high level of estrogen coupled with a low level of progesterone. This imbalance can lead to a variety of classic PMS symptoms, including binge eating. Eating disorders exacerbate PMS, which in turn fuels the eating disorder behavior.

The whole-person approach to PMS looks to the estrogen cycle. When your body produces estrogen, a B vitamin called choline converts the estrogen to estrone, which is then converted into estriol. Estriol, the substance remaining after the transformation process, is known to protect women against cancer. Estrogen, in its unconverted form, is responsible for the growth of many breast cysts leading to breast cancer. Your body is a finely tuned instrument: In one form, estrogen can be harmful, leading to cancer; in another form, estrogen can serve as a defense against cancer. Eating disorders disturb this delicate balance.

A daily supplement of nutrients, such as B-vitamin choline, can significantly reduce PMS symptoms, as can altering your overall diet. Eating properly can have profound effects on any PMS symptoms you're experiencing. Try complex carbohydrates such as vegetables, fruits, and grains. Reduce the amount of processed foods you consume, which often contain high amounts of fats, sugars, and simple carbohydrates. Instead, enjoy eating whole grains, fruits and vegetables, eggs, and legumes (beans). Replace animal fats with olive or peanut oil (be aware if you have a food sensitivity to peanuts, however). Several vitamins also aid in the detoxification of estrogen, particularly vitamin C, vitamin E, and selenium. All dietary modifications, however, should be done in consultation with a qualified nutritionist, dietitian, or physician.

We use a specialized formula called *Estrobalance* that we've found to be very helpful for those with an eating disorder and PMS. In addition, many of our female clients, with or without an eating disorder, have found progesterone creams to be highly effective in relieving premenstrual symptoms and reducing the severity of food cravings.

Birth Control Pills

One other area of concern for women is birth control pills. I've already stated that birth control pills contribute to the incidence of candida. They change the acid-alkaline balance of the vagina and can cause mood changes such as pessimism, irritability, fatigue, depression, and loss of sex drive. If you're taking birth control pills, it is vital that you eat a nourishing diet and supplement it with vitamins and minerals. Besides *Canditrol,* mentioned previously, I also recommend a supplement called *Stress B Plus,* which replenishes the B vitamin lost to birth control pills.

The whole-person approach takes into account these physical conditions of candida, hypoglycemia, food sensitivities, and PMS. Your eating disorder may have started as a *behavior,* but it can quickly become a *physical condition* as well. By treating your biochemistry and recognizing its effects, both positive and negative, your body can be allowed to do what it was intended to do—aid in your quality of life, not complicate the healing process of your mind. When body and mind work in harmony, as God intended, your process of healing will be greatly enhanced.

FOOD FOR THOUGHT

Am I Suffering from One or More of These Conditions?

Sometimes it's hard to know if you're experiencing any of these conditions and, if you are, what that means. Look over the following list of symptoms, and answer yes or no to each. They'll help you determine if you're suffering from any or all of the conditions discussed previously. Remember to be honest with your answers. When it comes to answering questions about our bodies, we often try to minimize what we're feeling. Don't do that here.

Candida
• I experience a constant pain in my body, especially in my digestive tract.
• I often feel depressed.

- I have had suicidal urges.
- My sex drive has diminished significantly.
- I am often constipated.
- I often have diarrhea.
- I have ulcers, gastritis, chronic indigestion, or abdominal bloating.
- I have experienced blurred vision.
- I am often lightheaded or dizzy. I often feel giddy.
- I have taken tetracycline or other antibiotics for acne for one month or longer.
- I have been bothered by persistent prostatitis, vaginitis, or other problems affecting my reproductive system.
- I have taken prednisone or other cortisone-type drugs for more than two weeks.
- I have taken birth control pills for over six months.
- I have an unpleasant reaction to perfumes, insecticides, fabric-shop odors, or other chemical odors.
- My symptoms are worse on damp or humid days or in damp or moldy places.
- I have had athlete's foot, ringworm, jock itch, or other chronic fungal infections of the skin or nails.
- My infections have been severe or persistent.
- I regularly crave sugar.
- I often crave breads.
- I regularly crave alcohol.

Because candida does not always show itself outwardly, you need to carefully consider your "yes" responses to see if there is any indication that you may be suffering from this yeast infection. Certain key outside influences, such as prolonged use of antibiotics, cortisone, or birth control pills, may have promoted candida within your system.

Hypoglycemia

- I go from having a lot of energy to being completely exhausted.
- I often feel depressed.
- When I feel bad, I eat something with a lot of sugar in it to make me feel better.
- If I get up from a seated position suddenly, I get dizzy and light-headed.
- I seem to be tired all of the time.
- I can't seem to make decisions very easily.
- I have trouble sleeping at night.
- During the day I have periods of time when I just can't seem to concentrate.
- I feel hungry between meals or at night.
- I wake up at night after only a few hours' sleep.
- I have trouble concentrating.
- I am often moody.
- I have feelings of intense anger or rage.
- I eat candy and drink soda or coffee between meals and in the mid-afternoon.
- I eat a lot of bread, pasta, potatoes, rice, or beans.
- I drink more than three cups of coffee or cola per day.
- I have headaches.
- I feel drowsy or sleepy after meals.
- I feel a lack of energy during the day.
- I feel revived by eating.
- I get irritable before I eat.
- I get shaky when I'm hungry.
- I can become faint if I don't eat right away.
- I have cold hands and/or feet.
- My hands tremble or shake.

While there could be contributing factors to some of these statements, if you answered yes to more than a third of these, a problem with hypoglycemia could very well be affecting your ability to function. You'll need to give serious consideration to treating this condition in conjunction with your eating disorder.

Food Sensitivities
- I often feel depressed.
- I get very drowsy during the day.
- I am tired all of the time.
- I have trouble learning new things.
- I often feel an unexplainable anxiety.
- At night, I just can't seem to fall asleep.
- Often I seem to be "supercharged."
- My memory isn't what it used to be, and I have trouble concentrating.
- I experience quick personality changes.
- Sometimes I find myself just wanting to be alone.
- Other times I get so angry I want to yell at someone.
- I get very dizzy.
- I experience hot flashes.
- I seem to be confused often.
- I have frequent headaches.
- I have experienced seizures.
- Sometimes I have trouble catching my breath.
- Sometimes I find myself wheezing or coughing.
- I have a problem with hyperventilation.
- I seem to need to go to the bathroom a lot, especially at night.
- It is painful to urinate.
- My periods are painful.
- My periods are irregular.

If you answered yes to several of these statements, you could be suffering from food sensitivities. By changing your diet, you can significantly improve the way you are feeling. It's important to ask yourself, however, if you really know everything you're eating. A nutritionist can help you chart your food intake and make needed changes.

Premenstrual Syndrome

- Before my period I experience severe cramping.
- I often become highly irritable around my period.
- I often become depressed before my period.
- My body tissues retain several pounds of water prior to my period.
- During my period I feel extremely fatigued.
- I experience severe headaches before my period.

IN THE RIGHT DIRECTION

KNOWING YOUR BODY

Right now, you may be experiencing a sense of relief—not because you're happy about having any of these conditions, but because you now realize that there are real physical reasons for your eating behaviors. Be careful, however, that you don't fall into the trap of denying the other conditions that contribute to your eating disorder. Usually you don't starve yourself or binge and purge because you are allergic to wheat flour. Your physical symptoms are probably the result of your eating disorder; they didn't start it.

Besides a sense of relief, you may also be feeling just a little put out with your body. You may even be seeing your own body as an enemy—an unyielding taskmaster demanding to be fed, expecting to be thin, and now sabotaging your mind's efforts to get well. Remember: Body and mind cannot be separated, nor should they be.

Just as these conditions didn't begin your eating disorder, treating them alone will not stop your faulty response to food. This book is not just another self-help book leading to the conclusion that all you have to do to be cured is stop eating sugar. Don't allow yourself to be sidetracked.

Your body is not your enemy, and neither are your thoughts and memories. This issue isn't about confrontation; it's about reconciliation. It's about reintegrating your whole person, mind and body.

(We invite you to call our toll-free number listed at the back of this book if you would like more information about the special formulas we use to assist those suffering from eating disorders. In addition, our Web site offers monthly "Hope Subscription" tapes, which cover topics related to eating disorders and nutritional recovery.)

AFFIRMING ACTION

God did not create the mind and body to be at war with each other. Rather, he perfectly crafted the human body as a temple for the human spirit. An eating disorder produces an unholy conflict between mind and body.

But God has shown himself over and over to be a God of reconciliation. He reconciles sinners to himself through Christ. He reconciles relationships between people through his love. And he has the power to reconcile your mind and your body back into the perfect vessel he created for your beautiful spirit.

With God's help I am loving myself and allowing peace between my mind and my body. I am healing.

Jean's Story

In the midst of my eating disorder, I lost track of life itself. I lost track of just plain living.

If there is one thing I can share with you, it is that there is hope. And hope is a gradual process. It won't be easy, but if you're willing to try, and continue to try day after day, you will make progress. Put your trust in something other than the eating disorder and begin to look at each day as a new day and a new start.

I think my turning point came when I put my eating disorder in the trust of my therapist, allowing my therapist to help me follow a food plan and gain weight. My weight still bothers me. I do yearn for the way my thin body felt, at times, but have come far enough to know that it was not healthy. I don't know if I'll ever be totally comfortable with my weight. I think it's more about accepting my body, not my weight.

I have learned I am stronger than I think and that strength isn't in staying thin, but in getting healthy. I know it is only through God's grace and love for me that I am still alive today and able to share my thoughts. I still have much work left to do to turn my life around and undo the circumstances from the past, but I know I am on the right path now.

My faith in God continues to grow. I know I must continue to lay aside my pride and put my trust in him daily. He can do wonderful things in my life, but I must first surrender and allow him. I have learned that God is my only hope and he is there for me always. He loves me and wants to provide for me. He can help me through anything and will never allow me more than

I can handle. I need to learn to turn to him before I turn to my other destructive defenses as a way to cope.

God is right here for us, and he will give us the desire, hope, and will that we need to take the first steps.

—Jean

Nine

Loving Yourself
from the Inside Out

"After all, no one ever hated his own body, but he feeds and cares for it, just as Christ does the church," the pastor said, quoting Ephesians 5:29.

At this point in the sermon, Karen stopped listening. The lesson continued, but she traveled off into a swirling eddy of memories and thoughts triggered by that passage.

After all, no one ever hated his own body...

Not hating your body was stated as a simple aside, as if the concept itself were a given. But it wasn't a given to Karen. Even now, she fought to remember that God expected her to love her body.

Her *body.* She was expected to love her *body.* This verse wasn't talking about her mind or her soul or her intellect. It specifically said "body"—her flesh, her bones, her hair and teeth. Her legs and arms. Even her breasts, her hips, her thighs.

There was a time in her life when the thought of loving her body had been as foreign to her as grace. For years, Karen hated her body with an active, punishing hate accompanied by action. She hated how she looked. She hated who she was. She hated who others wanted her to be. That hatred fueled the need to deprive her body of any sort of compassion.

After all, no one ever hated his own body, but he feeds and cares for it...

For several years, Karen had chosen not to feed or care for her body. Instead, she starved it into submission. With an iron will she resisted its attempts at self-preservation. The more she hungered, the less she ate. When she subjugated hunger, she took on thirst. Every bite, every sip, was done with elaborate calculation and extreme prejudice. She resented her body and its needs. It felt unclean to her. Starvation was pristine—no consumption, no elimination.

In Karen's midtwenties, her anorexia turned into bulimia. No longer able to beat her hunger and thirst into submission, she indulged it beyond measure. Oh, Karen fed her body—but only for a little while. Until she purged and felt clean again.

All through this time, Karen had loved God. But often she also feared him and felt distant from him. Yet she clung to the promise of his love, even as she struggled with loving herself. Slowly she was awakening to the thought of actually caring *for* herself, instead of only caring *about* herself.

Karen was striving to know God and to trust his expectations.

DAMAGE TO THE FLESH

Your body is paying a heavy price for your eating disorder. If you are bulimic and use laxatives or vomiting to purge, your skin is probably quite dry and frequently breaks out in small rashes and pimples. If your salivary glands haven't yet become enlarged because of your constant vomiting, they could.

If you're bulimic or anorexic, you probably experience continual constipation and intestinal bloating because you either don't keep down enough food to pass through your system or simply don't eat enough to trigger elimination. You may also have swollen, puffy hands and feet brought about by an electrolyte imbalance. For anorexics, this is because of malnutrition; for bulimics, vomiting or laxative abuse. If you compulsively overeat, your extra weight is putting a strain on nearly all your body's systems and setting you up for future health problems. These are not easy things to say or read, but you need to know the truth.

Your eating disorder today will affect your body tomorrow. One such effect is the slowing down of your metabolism. You have a unique metabolic rate that has become unbalanced by your lifestyle choices. Down the road, this can result in weight problems years after your eating disorder has been overcome. Your body can readjust itself in time, but the longer you continue in this destructive behavior, the more difficult it will be for your body to reestablish its proper functions.

If you are an anorexic woman, your self-starvation will lead to a complete loss of your menstrual period, if it hasn't already. Rigorous exercise, emotional ups and downs, even bingeing and purging can also shut down your body's reproductive systems. It knows something is wrong, even if you don't, and it's not about to take any chances with pregnancy. With menstrual loss comes estrogen loss, resulting in loss of calcium to your bones. Too much calcium loss can result in osteoporosis, or brittle-bone disease, later in life. Many young anorexics develop the bones of an eighty- or ninety-year-old.

If you're bulimic, the bitter acid from gastric juices washes over your teeth when you vomit and destroys enamel that can never be replaced. If you continue your eating habits long enough, your teeth will be irreparably damaged and will require either caps or replacement by dentures. What teeth you retain will be more susceptible to cavities because of weakened enamel.

If you use laxatives to purge, either exclusively or in addition to vomiting, there is added damage to your digestive system and bowels. If your body hasn't had to work at passing food through your system for a number of years, it has become lazy, and you'll need bulk lubricants to aid in having bowel movements.

If you are anorexic and are denying your body the life-sustaining nutrients it needs, your body will begin to turn on you. It will feed on itself in order to survive. When fat is no longer available, your body will begin to digest its own muscle tissue. Since your heart is a muscle, damage to this organ can become irreparable, even fatal. Your hair will thin and fall out.

Your eating disorder is putting an enormous stress on your body. Stress has been shown to have far-reaching effects, contributing to cancer and heart disease.

In light of these facts, it is vitally important that you begin to work on the reasons why you're engaging in this destructive behavior and begin to treat its physical effects. This is important not only for today but also for your tomorrow.

DAMAGE TO THE SPIRIT

Studies are yielding evidence that eating disorders don't just cause damage to the body's physical systems; they can also take a toll on the body's psychic systems. Those with an eating disorder may develop mood and anxiety disorders, such as depression, obsessive compulsive disorder, personality disorders, and substance abuse disorders.

I have witnessed, over my years of counseling, the coupling of an eating disorder with these other disorders. While healing can—and does—occur even when multiple disorders are present, the joining together of more than one disorder requires greater effort to overcome. I have also witnessed how healing from an eating disorder has assisted many people in overcoming other disorders. Just as damage from one weakens a person and can allow other disorders, healing from one strengthens a person and can prevent other disorders.

In every way, eating disorders promise short-term fixes and lead to long-term damage to mind and body.

A Change in Focus

Up to this point, your eating disorder has centered your focus on your outside appearance. You have focused on your desire to be thin. As such, your life has revolved around diets and weight. But inside is where you really live. The body is just a shell—a perishable one, at that—which God fully intends to replace. It is your inside, your spirit, that lasts forever. And this obsession with controlling the body is imprisoning your spirit.

The terrible irony of an eating disorder is that the damage being done to the inside, in the name of the outside, will eventually migrate to the outside. Healing comes when you decide to refocus your efforts from diets and weight (the outside) to nutrition and support for your body (the inside). You need to mentally go from food as friend, or food as fat, to food as nutrition. It can be extremely difficult to make this mental jump on your own. You may need to start with a spiritual refocusing.

Self-hate argues against the truth of God's love for you and the great value you have. It blinds you to an awareness of the beauty of God's creation that lies uniquely in you. The negative inner messages of self-hate deafen your ability to hear God's voice singing over you as a precious, valued human being. You can decide to stop listening to your self-hate and decide to hear the truth of God's love for you.

Wonderfully Made

Psalm 139:14 states, "I praise you because I am fearfully and wonderfully made; your works are wonderful, I know that full well."

Do *you* know that full well? Have you been treating your body as a wonderful work of God? God designed your body as a beautiful, complex system to support your life and give you great joy. The eating disorder is attacking that system and robbing the joy that God desires you to have. Just as some past mistakes in your life can have consequences that continue for years after the event, the damage you are doing now can affect the quality of your life for years after your recovery.

Recovery is possible. Remember that your body is quite resilient and forgiving. Much of the damage you have done is reparable with time and the proper nutritional support. But just as the process of your eating disorder took years to manifest its full damaging effects, so also your healing process will take time to accomplish. The sooner you start to repair this damage, the better—for your health, for your peace of mind, and for your very life.

FOOD FOR THOUGHT

Your Body's Survival

If you continue with your eating disorder, one very possible outcome might be death. Take some time to think about your own death. To help you do this, we have included an obituary below, just like one you would find in your local newspaper. Suppose tomorrow someone were to pick up that newspaper and read your obituary. What would you like it to say? Write your own obituary by completing these sentences. Do this only with a supportive person with you.

> One of our local residents, _____, died yesterday at the age of _____. She (He) is survived by…
>
> At the time of her (his) death, (s)he was attempting to achieve…
>
> Those who were close to her (him) will miss her (him) greatly because (s)he was the kind of person who…
>
> The thing (s)he was most proud of accomplishing in her (his) life was…
>
> Regretfully, her (his) dream of _____ was never fulfilled.

1. As I was writing my obituary, it made me feel…

2. When I think of my own death, it makes me feel scared, because I…

3. My own death fills a need for revenge against _____, because…

4. Part of me wants to die because…

   The rest of me wants to live because…

Wanting to get better means wanting to live. You must want to live. You must want to get better. You must want to experience the fullness of God's love for you. As you acknowledge your fear, fight for your faith—in your God, in yourself, in those you love. This acknowledgment will take courage, but you must be brave.

How would you be living today if you were brave?

5. Look at the equation below. Where are you? Where are your biggest gains?

Courage + Knowledge + Growth + Consistent Efforts = Recovery = Healing = Happiness

Decide now that recovery, healing, and happiness are worth the journey. If you need a second opinion, ask the Lord.

IN THE RIGHT DIRECTION

THE WONDER OF YOU

You are wonderfully unique beyond what you've been able to see. Each of us is a work of art, beautiful in our complexity. As children we experience an innate sense that we are good, that life is good, and that we are special. Somewhere along the line, however, through the actions of others and circumstances we can neither control nor comprehend, that self-awareness gets sidetracked. We stop seeing ourselves as "good" and start believing that we are in some way "bad." We don't really understand why we are bad, but we certainly know the results of our deficiency.

Things that have no value are not taken care of. Objects of great worth are cared for, protected, and prized. It is time to stop thinking of yourself as someone of no value. If you are having trouble finding that value on your own, look outside of yourself to friends, to caring family, and to God.

Being prized and protected, however, does not mean being pampered or permitted everything. There is a balance to be struck. Food should not be used as a reward. Your relationship with food can be a peaceful one.

Each act in the present has its consequences in the future. Acts of destruction will reap future damage, but acts of concern will produce healing. It's time for your reconstruction. With God's help and your determination, rebuilding can be done.

AFFIRMING ACTION

Recovery from an eating disorder—reconstruction—is an "inside-out" job. And the job is not complete until you have cleaned out emotionally, physically, and spiritually. As you are working at recovery, be aware that you may be tempted to "recycle" your eating disorder instead of getting rid of it completely. In times of stress, you may want to "recycle" back into old patterns. Expect this and prepare for it.

How do you prepare for it? Prayer is your best weapon in this effort to rid yourself of your eating disorder. Through prayer, you connect with the power of God to assist you in your determination to reclaim the beauty of God's creation that is you. Through prayer, you can hear God's voice reaffirm his care, concern, and love for you—now and in the future.

Dear God, I've been existing in the stagnation of my eating disorder, living from moment to moment in destructive obsession. I want to be free! I will reclaim the joy of faith in the future. Help me to see beyond today.

Thank you for helping me refocus my thoughts on the inward beauty of your creation. I will to see myself as someone lovely, valuable, and precious. Thank you for helping me love myself.

Ten

Reclaiming the Gift of Health

Sunlight slowly tracked across the bedroom floor to rest on top of Amanda's bed. There, it settled and warmed the comforter, waiting. Before long, Amanda stretched and blinked her eyes, coming into wakefulness.

It's morning, she thought, slightly amazed. *I must have slept through the night.* Perfectly still, Amanda lay there, trying to remember the last time she had actually slept all the way through the night. It was such an odd feeling, like time stood still.

Stretching some more, she realized she felt rested. Her bones didn't ache. *How long has it been?* she wondered. No headache. No upset stomach. No night terrors. No night sweats. No joint pain. No exhaustion. No wrestling with sleep all night long, only to awaken the next morning feeling like the loser.

This is what peace feels like, she told herself. It was decadent.

For too long, Amanda had been at war with sleep. It never surrendered without a fight. It capitulated only in the face of abject exhaustion, and then for mere brief snatches of time. Even when she drugged herself into oblivion, there was still the vague acknowledgment of muscles that cramped, intestines that bloated, mouth and nasal passages that dried and cracked. Sleep was not about rest; it was about survival. She needed sleep to survive, and the bare minimum was all she was ever allowed by her eating disorder.

Night was not a time to relax; it was a time to be on guard. Left alone with the pounding of her heart, Amanda had spent far too many nights huddled in bed, tense, anxiously awaiting the next thump, wondering if this was the night her body would spiral out of control altogether. Often, panic would pounce, sending her pulse racing and chilling her feet like ice, while she broke out in a sweat, terrified. Sleep had not been sweet for a very long time. Her eating disorder had robbed her of rest for more years than she cared to count.

Yet here she was, on this quiet morning, experiencing a rare moment of tranquility. *I used to be able to sleep like this,* she reminded herself, thinking back to childhood and the cheery mornings she'd awakened in her warm bed, full of thoughts no deeper than what game to play with her sister after breakfast.

It's been a long time, she thought, tears coming to her eyes. *I want to be able to fall asleep and wake up refreshed like this every morning. I want to be able to concentrate on living instead of fixating on dying. I want to start the day with hope and not dread.*

I want to wake up in the morning and be glad.

RECLAIMING REST

Eating disorders wreak havoc with the natural rhythms of your body. If you are anorexic, sleep is more akin to a physical shutdown due to a lack of energy. Without nutrients, the body is unable to be proactive in sleep, repairing damage done at the cellular level. If you are bulimic, sleep is interrupted by the aftereffects of purging—continual diarrhea if on laxatives or a digestive system in upheaval if vomiting. If you are an overeater, your digestive system never has a time to rest; it is constantly working to process the excessive amounts of food you force through it. When your body is your battlefield, there are no moments of peace.

During the day, activities and the pace of life can mask the physical effects of your eating disorder. You can stay busy enough to be distracted. But at night, the truth makes itself known. At night, with just you and your body, the physical imbalances caused by your eating disorder scream out into the silence, making sleep difficult, if not impossible.

A body out of balance cannot experience restorative sleep, and a lack of sleep produces a body out of balance. Round and round it goes. Besides, how can you remain hopeful when you are constantly depleted and exhausted? This is the key reason why a whole-person approach to healing includes returning the body to a healthy balance.

RECLAIMING HEALTH

This probably isn't the first book you've picked up to help you get a handle on your eating disorder. It's probably only one of many. If you're like most people with eating disorders, you've got a shelf full of self-help and diet books.

And it doesn't stop with books. You listen for any explanation of what's wrong with you and then run out to buy the latest vitamin or dietary supplement. If you hear that potassium is the answer to your problem, you buy a bushel of bananas. Your cabinet is probably full of vitamins and supplements—and your stool is probably full of those same vitamins. Your body is so out of balance that it can't make use of the good things you do give it.

You need to recognize that this desire for a quick fix—even one intended to correct the physical consequences of your eating disorder—is part of your pattern of avoidance. What is required is not a secret diet program, a magic pill, a perfect drug, or a miracle supplement that is going to make all of your physical symptoms go away. Rather, what is required is a lifelong commitment to giving your body what it needs to be healthy—not giving your body only what you want to give it to be comforted.

Let me say that again: An eating disorder is a war between what your body needs to be healthy and what you want to give it to be comforted or to feel powerful. For an anorexic, giving it very little (or nothing) is comforting, but it destroys the body. For a bulimic, purging is comforting, but it depletes the body. For a bulimic or an overeater, bingeing is comforting, but it pollutes the body. Food is not about comfort; food is about nutrition.

When a person with an eating disorder comes to me, I don't ask what he or she is eating, nor do I tell people what they should eat. Generally, people already know what they *need* to be eating to be healthy. What is getting in the way is what they *want* to be eating or not eating. Besides, if I started out by listing what you can and cannot eat, it would sound suspiciously like a diet. You've probably already done your own categorizing of "good" and "bad" foods; you don't need me to add to that.

I am not—repeat, *not*—going to suggest you go on a diet. What's the first thing you want to do on a diet? Why, rebel, of course. Diets represent force and control. But force is not an effective tool for treating an eating disorder, and control only reinforces the eating disorder. Instead, I present information about how wonderful our bodies are, and I work with each person to develop an appreciation for how the body best functions. Together, we work to put this knowledge into perspective with what is being learned about the behavioral aspects of the eating disorder. We work to integrate whole-person understanding and, with it, healing.

Not everyone who treats eating disorders approaches healing through a dedicated emphasis on nutrition. And this chapter is not meant to downplay other approaches. Instead, it is meant to highlight what I have found to be an extremely effective approach over years of treating eating disorders. I have been privileged to witness not only rebuilt lives but rebuilt bodies. My experience is that when one supports the other, healing is heightened and recovery is long-term.

Rebuilding Digestion

To start your body's rebalancing process, you must rebuild your digestion. After all, if you are unable to digest what you need to rebalance your system, what you take to rebalance it will have little value. The first step to rebuilding your digestion is to reestablish your digestive system's natural acid-alkaline, or pH, balance. A healthy digestive system contains an abundance of bacteria called *flora,* of which the most commonly known is acidophilus. Acidophilus requires the correct pH balance to thrive.

Within a balanced pH environment, healthy digestive bacteria flourish and provide the mechanism to break down the substances you eat into components your body can absorb and use. Likewise, digestive enzymes allow food to be broken down into its component parts for easy absorption and a reduction in intestinal bloating and gas. When your digestive enzyme level is out of whack, healthy flora can't grow; unhealthy organisms, like the yeast candida, make opportune use of this imbalance. Faulty digestion also affects mood and energy levels. If your stomach is upset, you get irritable and fatigued.

Dairy products with active yogurt cultures contain acidophilus, as do other milk products. Acidophilus milk is milk that has been fermented by bacteria and used therapeutically to change intestinal flora. Check your local grocery store for these products. Many of the clients we work with have found it a tremendous benefit to augment the acidophilus found in dairy products with a special formula called *Ultra Flora Plus*. This formula contains billions of active acidophilus bacteria and is taken as a dietary supplement.

Another important step to rebuilding your digestion is the reintroduction of adequate fiber, to keep your elimination system regular. Most eating disorder clients are extremely constipated and may not realize it. We use *Phase Four*, a non-caloric, high-fiber, special bulk formula extremely helpful for both anorexics and bulimics.

Reintroduction of adequate fiber is especially important when there has been laxative abuse. The bowels need to relearn how to function again. I have helped countless clients with *Phase Four* after they had been told by others that their systems would never function properly again.

Nutritional Rehabilitation

Once the digestive system is functioning properly again, vitamins and other nutritional formulas can be reintroduced, because you will be able to assimilate them. Then is the time to begin taking potassium and zinc. The preferred form of potassium is potassium chelate in a powder capsule form. If you are still purging, wait at least an hour to purge after taking potassium. When you allow yourself to wait an hour after consuming something, you may find that your desire to get rid of the food is reduced. Because your stomach is learning to work properly again, you may find yourself thinking, *I'm feeling better. I think I might be okay.* Learn to trust the process.

Along with potassium, zinc must also be reintroduced in proper levels. A lack of zinc impairs the ability to smell and taste. When zinc levels have been increased in women suffering from anorexia, all reported an increase in appetite and renewed ability to experience taste.

Next comes the introduction of the B vitamins, along with amino acids. Amino acids are especially important to you, because they affect your hunger and your desire to sleep. The improper balance of amino acids can lead to depression, sleeplessness, fatigue, lack of hunger, or intense cravings. Many clients I work with have excellent results from a formula called *Ultra Meal.* It is a highly digestible, quickly assimilated protein source. There are no sugars or additives in *Ultra Meal,* and it is formulated to contain the nutrients for a complete meal. This powdered supplement can be taken alone or mixed with yogurt or fruit in a blender. It is also delicious when combined with crushed ice to produce a frothy, nutritious drink. In addition, we have specially formulated B-complex vitamins and multivitamin formulas available.

A word of caution here about powdered "nutrition" drinks. Some of the most popular brands on the market are not recommended for those with eating disorders. They contain high levels of sugar, even though the label may not make it clear. (There are a number of names for sugar, usually with an *ose* suffix, such as glucose, dextrose, and sucrose.) These drinks can also be difficult to digest for someone with an eating disorder and may have lower nutrient contents than I recommend for those with eating disorders.

Along with the B vitamins already mentioned, there are a variety of other vitamins essential to proper digestion and physiological functioning:

- *Vitamin A.* This vitamin aids in maintaining the proper functioning of the mucous membranes of the mouth, noise, throat, lungs, ears, and other organs. It aids in vision, especially in dim light. It is necessary for healthy skin, bones, and teeth. Symptoms of vitamin A deficiency are night blindness, roughness and dryness of skin, drying of mucous membranes, and digestive problems.

- *Thiamine (Vitamin B₁).* Thiamine helps change glucose into energy or fat, assists oxygen distribution to the body, aids in digestive functioning, and helps maintain proper functioning of the nervous system and cardiovascular system. Symptoms of thiamine deficiency are fatigue, as well as digestive difficulties: constipation, flatulence, and intestinal bloating.

- *Choline, Inositol, and B₆.* These vitamins aid in the production of blood and the use of fats. B₆ is vital to the normal functioning of the brain, nerves, and muscle tissue. These B vitamins also help maintain blood cholesterol at a healthy level. Nervousness, weakness, and lethargy are associated with a deficiency of these nutrients.

- *Riboflavin (Vitamin B₂).* In combination with vitamin A, riboflavin promotes good vision and healthy skin. It also assists in metabolizing proteins and fats at a cellular level, increasing tissue oxidation and respiration. One of the first symptoms of deficiency of this nutrient is a burning feeling in the eyes. Advanced symptoms include lesions in the mouth and on the lips, appearing as fissures or cracks radiating from the corners onto the skin.

- *Cyanocobalamin (Vitamin B₁₂).* This B vitamin aids in the functioning of cells in the nervous system, bone marrow, and intestinal tract, increasing metabolism of protein, carbohydrates, and fats. The most severe symptom of deficiency of cyanocobalamin is acute anemia.

- *Biotin (Vitamin H).* This vitamin also aids in metabolizing proteins, carbohydrates, and fats. Symptoms of deficiency include dry, peeling skin and depression.

- *Folic Acid.* Folic acid is necessary for cellular division and the production of RNA and DNA. It is also needed for the utilization of sugar and amino acids. Fatigue, dizziness, shortness of breath, and grayish-brown skin are all symptoms of deficiency.

- *Niacin.* Niacin is important for tissue respiration, brain and nervous system functioning, and healthy skin. Many symptoms of a deficiency of this nutrient appear as mental impairment, such as suspicion, irritability, loss of memory, insomnia, and anxiety. Physical symptoms can be abdominal pain, a burning sensation on the tongue, and dry and scaly skin, especially when exposed to sunlight.

- *Pantothenic Acid.* This aids in the release of energy from sugars and fats. It is important for adrenal gland functioning; without it, some nutrients cannot be metabolized. Deficiencies lead to fatigue, abdominal cramping, nausea, irritability, and depression.

- *Ascorbic Acid (Vitamin C).* This powerhouse vitamin is important to the body's connective tissues and for the development of healthy bones and teeth, cellular formation and maturation, resistance to infection, and an increased ability to heal. Scurvy is the primary symptom of deficiency, a disease associated with ancient seafarers who were unable to maintain proper levels of fresh fruit in their diets. Vitamin C deficiency is typified by bleeding gums, inability to heal or slow healing, loss of appetite, increased infections, and muscular weakness.

- *Vitamin D.* Vitamin D aids in the absorption, retention, and metabolizing of calcium. This is why vitamin D is added to milk products. When you do not have enough vitamin D, your bones and teeth are weakened. Deficiency in this nutrient can also be manifested in a weakened and flabby muscle structure.

Knowing what nutrients you need, and at what levels, can be a daunting task. For this reason, I have formulated a phased supplement system to allow those with eating disorders to gradually rebuild their nutritional balances. Each phase, from *Phase One* to *Phase Three,* is a specially designed nutritional system, beginning with those most compromised by an eating disorder and working toward restoration of nutritional health.

Healthy Choices

Working toward healthy choices and increased physiological health should be goals for everyone, not just those recovering from an eating disorder. Below, you will find recommendations adapted from the U.S. Department of Health and Human Services. These are excellent guidelines for long-term, healthy choices:

1. *Eat a variety of foods, even if in very small amounts.* This may seem simple, but it is of tremendous importance to anyone with an eating disorder. For many, certain foods have become associated with comfort or safety, while others are avoided as unsafe. As a result, food variety is lost.

2. *Balance the food you eat with physical activity.* Maintain or improve your weight. The key word here is balance. Physical activity is a wonderful companion to healthy eating, as long as the activity is in balance. For those who are underweight, the goal is to improve your weight by increasing it. For those who are overweight, the goal is to improve your weight by decreasing it. Physical activity also works to increase metabolism. Often, metabolism is slowed by an eating disorder.

3. *When making food choices, include plenty of grain products, vegetables, and fruit.* We live in a remarkable time when all these foods are readily available. This recommendation goes hand-in-hand with eating a variety of foods.

4. *Make food choices that are low in fat and cholesterol.* This advice is particularly helpful to those with bulimia or compulsive overeating. Many of the foods you choose for comfort may be extremely high in fat. Quick, processed fast foods are also high in fats.

5. *Make food choices that are moderate in sugar content.* Again, sweets and carbohydrates are often the binge foods of choice for bulimics and overeaters. Hypercharging your system with sugars increases

blood sugar, which results in an increase in the production of insulin. When insulin elevates, blood sugar drops, and appetite surges, perpetuating a cycle of bingeing.

6. *Make food choices that are moderate in salt content.* Many bulimics and overeaters will alternate between sweet and salty foods during a binge. Be aware of your eating patterns and whether you are establishing a pattern of alternating between sweet and salty.

7. *If you drink alcoholic beverages, do so in moderation.* Over half of my eating disorder clients misuse alcohol. For some, it has become a way of self-medicating, as it numbs both physical and emotional pains. For others, alcohol is considered a safe substance to ingest. Because compulsive behaviors may come in groups, those with eating disorders need to be especially careful of the potential for abusing alcohol through overconsumption.

To these recommendations, I would add one more: *Make food choices that are moderate in caffeine content.* Caffeine creates vitamin B deficiencies and can act as a masking agent for symptoms of eating disorders. In particular, anorexics will use caffeine as an energy booster in place of proper nutrition. Bulimics and overeaters will also use caffeine to counter fatigue and headaches brought on by a drop in blood sugar levels due to purging or an increase in insulin levels.

Avoiding Hypoglycemia

Hypoglycemia is best known as low blood sugar. It usually occurs in the late afternoon when insulin levels are elevated after lunch. Insulin counteracts blood sugar, causing fatigue. Those who suffer from hypoglycemia will often take a short nap in the afternoon or have a light snack before dinner. Hypoglycemia, in a person with an eating disorder, can induce a raging desire to binge—consuming extreme amounts of calories.

Those with an eating disorder can be especially susceptible to hypoglycemia. Most eating disorder clients I have worked with are hypoglycemic. Eating disorders produce stress, and stress can result in hypoglycemia due to an overactive adrenal gland. When too much sugar or carbohydrates are eaten, the pancreas gets used to dumping increased amounts of insulin into the blood system. As insulin levels rise, hypoglycemia is the result. Severe restriction of food can also produce the weakness associated with hypoglycemia, as can inadequate levels of the minerals calcium, magnesium, potassium, phosphate, and the trace elements manganese, zinc, and chromium. In fact, chromium is essential in the proper utilization of glucose, allowing the body to use the minimum amount of insulin necessary to maintain proper blood sugar levels.

These minerals assist your body in regulating blood sugar levels. By maintaining the proper levels of these minerals, you can help your body avoid the ups and downs of hypoglycemia and hyperglycemia, also known as elevated blood sugar.

Food Allergies and Sensitivities

Colic was once brushed off as "just a fussy baby." Now, however, colic is looked upon as a symptom of an immature digestive system and can signal a propensity for food allergies. Many of the eating disorder clients I have seen were colicky as babies and, as adults, have come to recognize an allergy to such foods as wheat and dairy products. Ironically, the foods most craved by those with an eating disorder are often their allergic foods.

We help clients to match certain foods with specific symptoms. Most are unaware they have sensitivities to food or food allergies. These may have developed over the years of the disorder, often the result of bingeing with the same foods over and over. In the dreadful cycle of bulimia, binge foods develop into sensitivities and allergies and then become the foods the bulimic will most crave, worsening the cycle. It can be difficult to stop.

Over the years, we have seen tremendous results when clients significantly reduce foods associated with allergic reactions. These clients are able to reduce their number and severity of colds, moderate their moods, reduce seasonal allergies, and, importantly, reduce the incidence and severity of binge behaviors.

Premenstrual Syndrome and Premenopausal Symptoms

In the ebb and flow of the menstrual cycle, nutrients and hormonal levels fluctuate. This natural fluctuation can be especially distressing to a woman with an eating disorder. Because her system is already off-balance, her menstrual cycle can send it tottering even further, intensifying feelings of depression, irritability, bloating, and heightening food cravings. In addition, the stress an eating disorder puts on the body can cause irregular menstrual cycles, heightening symptoms of PMS.

The hormonal fluctuations of the menstrual cycle can be especially stressful for anorexics who, due to loss of body fat, go into a premenopausal state. Menopause, in and of itself, is a time of heightened stress for the body as the adrenal glands decrease production of estrogen and progesterone. The body must adjust. In this time of menstrual transition, periods fluctuate wildly. Being irregular, they can produce many of the symptoms listed above, as well as night sweats, severe mood swings, and fatigue.

In order to assist women with these symptoms, we utilize enhanced nutrition, increased fiber consumption, appropriate exercise, and a highly absorbable progesterone cream called *Profeminell.* Many of our eating disorder clients have had great success moderating their premenstrual and premenopausal symptoms through the use of this progesterone cream.

Detoxifying Your Body

If you have an eating disorder, your body will tend to be very toxic. In other words, your body has become polluted through taking in the wrong substances or not taking in the correct ones. It has become polluted through its inefficiency in processing the food you do eat.

If you are anorexic, you will often eat only one type of food when you choose to eat at all. Neither bulimics nor anorexics take in the proper foods needed to cleanse the system of toxic build-up. In addition, when candida is present, it pours toxicity into the body as a natural byproduct of the yeast growth cycle.

Because of this, I suggest an aid to assist in colon cleansing, or "flushing out" your system, called *Phase Four*. It's made of psyllium, a natural fiber that absorbs toxins. *Phase Four* flushes through your system, cleaning out your colon. In addition, the psyllium present in this formula aids in the reduction of constipation. It allows the proper amount of liquid to be absorbed into your intestinal tract, promoting normal elimination.

If all of this seems confusing to you, relax. The phased nutritional formulas include complete instructions on how and when to take them and for how long. The initial formulas include digestive enzymes to reduce the bloated, uncomfortable feeling you will have when you begin to retain food again. The later stages help rebalance your body and its systems, while the last stage can be used to aid in normal bowel movements and cleansing.

When You Eat

When you eat can be as important as *what* you eat. Most of you know that breakfast is called the most important meal of the day. That is especially true for you. What you eat at breakfast can help determine the success of your day's eating pattern. *Ultra Meal,* mentioned previously, is an excellent choice for your morning meal. It contains amino acids, which help combat depression, and protein and fiber to stimulate your bowels. If you are hypoglycemic, breakfast can push your energy level up at the start of the day and help keep it that way, so that the desire to binge later on is lessened.

It's a good idea to consume the majority of your daily intake of food before early afternoon. You are more apt to burn up the calories you eat earlier in the day than those you eat later in the evening. If you are bulimic or a compulsive eater, you will also be less likely to binge if you eat the bulk of your food earlier in the day.

A SOUND NUTRITIONAL PROGRAM

I cannot overstress the importance of beginning a sound nutritional program in the early phases of treatment. When your physical body is supported, it can help you find the self-confidence and encouragement to deal with the important emotional, relational, and spiritual issues that need to be addressed for your long-term recovery.

Often people will come to me after going through a treatment program that leaves out the nutritional or physical component. They've failed, returning to or never totally giving up their behavior. Their guilt and feelings of frustration are tremendous. They're convinced that they must stop doing what they've been doing, but they seem powerless to make lasting changes. If you are willing to adopt a whole-person approach, your chances of success will be much greater.

Restoring nutritional balance requires patience on your part. I generally counsel clients to expect a minimum of three months—potentially longer, depending upon the type and severity of the eating disorder—before they will begin to see significant improvement.

There are a variety of opinions regarding the effectiveness of nutritional support for recovery from eating disorders. While I appreciate these differences, I can only stress what I have seen work in the lives of those I have counseled over the years. If you are working with a counselor or professional for your eating disorder and this aspect is not being addressed, we invite you to call us at our toll-free number for an eating disorder nutritional evaluation.

FOOD FOR THOUGHT

Coming Clean

The physical side effects of your disorder are not unlike the environmental complications that have arisen from pollution in our world today. You may have trouble imagining your body as polluted, so do the following exercise using graphic pictures that depict the damage pollution is causing to the earth.

1. Collect some magazines and make a collage of beautiful pictures of the earth: sky scenes, landscapes, seascapes. If you can't find appropriate images, draw a picture in your journal of a beautiful world. This world represents the way God intended your body to be.

2. Find pictures of the ravages of pollution. On the next page in your journal, draw or paste pictures of how pollution has harmed the world. These images represent how your eating disorder has polluted your body. Be aware of your physical reactions to these different pictures. Does the beautiful scenery make you feel calm and peaceful? Does the polluted world give you feelings of sadness?

3. At the bottom of each picture, write a brief description of how you feel about what you're looking at.

   Just as the awareness of pollution's dangers has caused people to repair the damage done to our earth, so also your own awareness of the real toll you are placing on your body can give you added motivation for discovering the source behind the pollution of your eating disorder and putting an end to it.

   Looking at the picture of the world (my body) as God intended it makes me feel...

   Looking at the picture of the world (my body) as it has been polluted makes me feel...

IN THE RIGHT DIRECTION

VIBRANT HEALTH IS YOUR GOAL

All your life you've heard the expression "It's never too late." You need to believe that now. Yes, there has been damage done to your body because of your eating disorder, but that damage can be dealt with and, in most cases, reversed.

In the past, you have spent a good deal of time focusing on how your body looks from the outside. Now it's time to look at your body from the inside. What is happening to you on the inside affects how you look on the outside. Your eating disorder has not brought you to the point of vibrant health. Instead, it is robbing you of your well-being, little by little.

Before, you were concerned only with the end result, attaining the "perfect" figure. Now you need to be concerned with the means you are using to that end and the damage they are causing. To be thin is not necessarily to be healthy. Vibrant health is what you are striving for physically. Proper nutrition can aid your body in regaining the health of its systems.

> Please go online to www.aplaceofhope.com/audio/nutrition.html
> for my special message on the healing benefits of nutrition.

If you've been in treatment programs that didn't address this aspect of your disorder, you may be a bit skeptical of the role nutrition can play in your recovery. All I ask is that you withhold judgment until you've tried it. By supporting your body nutritionally, you can aid your mind in conducting its healing work. When body and mind work together and support each other, the whole person benefits.

AFFIRMING ACTION

Consider these verses: "Don't you know that you yourselves are God's temple and that God's Spirit lives in you? If anyone destroys God's temple,

God will destroy him; for God's temple is sacred, and you are that temple" (1 Corinthians 3:16-17).

How long has it been since you considered your body a temple? Have you ever thought of yourself that way? God does. He considers your body as sacred. So sacred, he considers it an appropriate place for his Spirit to dwell.

In this world, you also are God's hands and his feet. You are part of the body of Christ.

Up to now, you have considered your body your own. You have decided that you can treat, or mistreat, your body however you choose. You may have given God your heart, your mind, your soul, and your strength—but you have withheld his sovereignty over your body. You have chosen to continue to conduct your eating disorder on a body that does not truly belong to you any longer.

Are you ready to give your body to God? Are you ready to submit to his will concerning your body? And what is his will? For you to recognize your body as his temple, sacred to him.

I am learning to trust my body to function and heal as God designed it to. I am learning to accept and love all of me...my body included.

Eleven

The Price of Anger

"Andrew, you've got to lose some weight." The words were coming out of the mouth of his doctor, but Andrew's mind heard someone else's voice quite clearly.

"Andrew, you've got to lose some weight," his mother announced to everyone at the dinner table. "You don't really need that second helping, now, do you?"

When would she stop picking on him in front of the family? It was always something. He didn't try hard enough in school. He didn't dress appropriately. He wasn't home on time. He didn't listen to her. He wasn't helpful around the house. He ate too much. On and on it went. Nothing he did seemed to stop her relentlessly negative comments.

And it wasn't just him. She complained about everyone else in the family. She complained about the clerk at the grocery store, the teller at the bank, the driver in the next car. She complained about the bills, the kids next door, the neighbor down the street. From the time she woke up to the time she went to bed, she wove an endless litany of complaints about anything and everything in her world. A recurring theme: She was overworked and under-appreciated.

She alone understood what needed to be done to make things right and had no tolerance for anyone who disagreed with her. Especially her family. And for some reason Andrew could never seem to catch hold of, she had no tolerance for him. His very presence seemed to drive her to extreme irritation, a lightning rod for her wide-ranging displeasure.

When he was younger, it hurt when she criticized him. As a teenager, it just made him angry. Going out for sports in high school helped. It gave him a way to vent his frustration and allowed him the luxury of eating just about anything he wanted. He was still large, but on the defensive front line it wasn't considered a negative. Whenever his mother commented on his weight, he just ate more. When she commented on his clothing, he dressed the same. When she commented on his comings and goings, he stayed out late. When she commented on his usefulness around the house, he shrugged and did nothing.

"Carrying that much weight, Andrew, just simply isn't healthy. It's putting a tremendous strain on your heart, on all your physical systems. Have you given serious thought to losing weight?" It was his doctor's voice again.

Oh, he'd given serious thought to it. In fact, he'd been thinking about his weight most of his life. Overeating had started as a way to declare his independence from all the negative comments thrust his way. As a teenager and young adult, though, he'd been mostly able to keep his weight in check. Somewhere down the road to adulthood, he'd lost the battle of the bulge and was now middle-aged and seriously overweight. And no matter what he tried, nothing seemed to help. The whole thing made him mad.

WHERE ANGER LEADS

If you suffer from an eating disorder, it is more than likely that you are not a happy person. The pain of your behavior has blocked out most of your ability to feel joy in life. Your emotions may have become so numbed by now that you rarely feel anything at all. Yet, while you think you feel nothing, negative emotions exist within you. They poison your ability to experience personal happiness. Their toxicity despoils life's simple pleasures.

You may have also become an isolated person. The shame of what you do causes you to withdraw from the company of others. You may feel that no one could possibly understand why you do what you do, so you don't even try to explain. Perhaps in an off-guard moment in the past, you made an attempt to communicate your feelings to someone, but that person reacted so badly that you never tried to talk about your disorder again. Without the free flow of personal interaction, you have become emotionally constipated.

Eating disorders begin with personal pain and set up a vicious cycle of anger: destructive behavior—shame—depression—self-hate—and back to anger. No matter what your eating disorder, the misuse of food starts as a natural response of anger to pain. It goes something like this:

- Something has caused tremendous pain in your life.
- The pain hurts, and that you should experience this pain is unjust and makes you angry.
- As you look for a way to vent this anger, to seek respite from the anger, you choose food.
- Abuse of food, either through over- or underconsumption, becomes a self-destructive behavior.
- Your active participation in a self-destructive behavior produces feelings of guilt and shame.
- Intense feelings of guilt and shame produce a profound sense of depression.
- Guilt, shame, and depression reinforce self-hate.
- Self-hate says you deserve the pain.
- Now you are angry not only at the pain in your past but at yourself for the pain in your present.
- Once again you chose to vent this anger, to gain relief from this anger, by abusing food and continuing your self-destructive behavior.
- Continuing this behavior produces shame and guilt.
- Shame and guilt reinforce self-hate.
- Self-hate says you deserve the pain.
- And so it goes.

The shame of your behavior, and the anger you feel by being pressured to conform to the image of how others want you to be, have driven you into a secret life. You have become an expert at deceiving others and yourself about what you eat, when you eat, and how much you eat. Food, instead of being a means of social interaction, has become a private, personal friend or foe.

It's not surprising, then, that you have become completely demoralized. Who would want to live this way? There's nothing pleasurable about starving yourself to death, gorging yourself beyond any measure of fullness, or bingeing and purging uncontrollably.

If you are bulimic, you are well aware that something is terribly wrong, and you've tried to change. Over and over again, you've promised yourself that you'll never do it again, but never only lasts until next time.

If you are anorexic, you may have been able to delude yourself into thinking that there's nothing wrong with the way you live your life. Deep inside, however, in the quiet moment of truth, you know perfectly well what you're doing. You may even know how it all began, but you don't know how to stop.

If you compulsively overeat, you have hidden yourself in food, pretending that there is no pain and that it doesn't matter. While you passively pretend the pain doesn't matter, your weight aggressively declares that it does.

ROUND AND ROUND IT GOES

Shadowing your eating disorder, like a wraith barely seen or acknowledged, is anger. Sometime in the past you've been deeply wounded. When we are hurt, our immediate reaction is one of anger. Whether the pain is a bashed thumb, causing us to cry out in rage at the hammer, or the taunting jibe of a trusted friend, getting hurt makes us mad.

The anger you've felt because of being hurt has been turned inward. For some reason you couldn't direct that anger at the person responsible for your pain, so it stayed within you. Anger, improperly directed and unexpressed, leads to resentment. Your resentment has festered into your self-destructive eating disorder.

Think back to the obituary you wrote in the "Food for Thought" section of chapter 9. Go back and reread the statement you wrote about revenge. At the bottom of your need for revenge is a desire to vent your feelings of anger at the person who hurt you.

Just as you did with the pain in your past, you also learned to transfer your anger to food. You used food to divert these feelings, to make the pain go away, to provide a way to forget the pain for a time. Eating certain foods actually made you feel better. Control of your body through food was a substitute for control over your anger.

This method of controlling your anger has not brought about the benefits you thought it would. It has left you a desperately unhappy person, unable to feel real joy in your life. It has stripped away your ability not only to express anger but also to experience emotions in general, leaving you to exist in a numbing limbo.

At first only the anger was expressed through your disorder, but now more and more feelings are dealt with through food or control of food. The predictable outcome of your disorder is a faulty sense of security. Any sort of stress, any uncertainty, can be dealt with through the sure and predictable pattern of your addiction. It has become your sole way of dealing with life.

IT'S TIME TO GET OFF

To begin to really live again and experience life with all its textures of emotion, you need to search back into your past and find the pain that caused your anger. You must find the pain, and you must find out who *caused* the pain. All your life you've been punishing yourself for the hurt caused by someone else. It's time to make the person who caused your pain responsible for it.

Often the people responsible for the pain are the people you love most—your parents. As any child who loves his or her parents would, you may have been shielding them from the responsibility for your pain by acting out your anger on yourself. But people need to be made responsible for the pain they cause. If they aren't, they are doomed never to learn from their actions, forced to repeat those actions over and over with you or someone else. Often the person who hurt you is not even aware of the magnitude, or even the existence, of the pain you feel. It's time they were told.

Most parents, when faced with the truth of their child's addiction, will not want the anger to stay with the child, causing further damage. When they raised you, they were probably doing it the best way they knew how. It's likely they did not understand at the time what you were feeling. Often parents become so absorbed in their own reactions they are unable to recognize and appreciate those of the child.

It's scary to anticipate this revelation of old anger and pain. If you thought you could tell your parents how you feel, then you probably would have done so already. If your feelings were never allowed free expression as a child, you may have great reluctance to be open in the present. Confrontation is rarely pleasant, but your pain needs to be expressed openly, honestly, and outwardly, no matter how far in the past it originated.

Along with confronting your anger and those responsible for it, you will also need to confront something else, an emotion inextricably linked to anger—sadness. Sadness over your fantasy of a perfect family being shattered; sadness over a childhood lacking in love and acceptance; sadness over not being able to go back and change what has happened; sadness over years of wrong choices you've made that have led to further pain.

It's time this anger and sadness are dealt with and put in their proper place. Ultimately, when you understand the pain, the anger, and the sadness behind the anger, the time will come for you to confront, to forgive, and to go on with your life.

ALL BY MYSELF

But anger is a jealous lover; it desires to consume your every waking thought. An eating disorder is similarly consuming. When anger is teamed with an eating disorder, there is very little room left for joy, peace, contentment, acceptance. There is very little room left for other people.

Eating disorders produce a certain level of social isolation, anger tends to finish the job, and shame takes up any bit that's left. It has been said that depression is anger turned inward. An eating disorder produces a similar folding-in on oneself. The pain, the anger, the abuse of food, all combine to overwhelm relationships, social interaction, or a healthy focus on others. There is no time to truly devote to others when the eating disorder literally takes up all your thoughts and energy.

You don't want to be around people because they don't understand or cooperate with your eating disorder. Other people don't want to be around you because they don't understand what you do or why you're so edgy all the time. This rejection by others is both resented by you and created by your actions. In order to reconnect with people, you will need to decide that you want to be with them more than you want to hold on to your anger and your eating disorder.

Letting people into your life means allowing them to know who you are, eating disorder and all. Those who love you will not sit quietly by while you engage in self-destructive behavior. They will plead with you, argue with you, cry with you, pray with you. But they will want you to change. And as they want you to change, this may aggravate your anger at those in your past who also wanted you to change in some way stated or implied, strengthening your rage.

In short, becoming more involved with people may intensify the pain. You must be prepared for this and accept the fact that confronting the pain, and the anger it has caused, is vital to your recovery. Yes, opening up will bring the hurt to the forefront where you can begin to deal with it, surrounded by those who love and care for you. Your eating disorder is blinding you to your pain, but those who love you see your pain quite clearly. They see it and they hurt for you. But you must not allow them to bear your hurt alone; you must accept your hurt for yourself. Accept it, understand it, begin to defuse it.

FOOD FOR THOUGHT

Understanding Anger

You've been numbing or avoiding your anger through your eating disorder for so long that it may be difficult for you to connect with that anger and put it into words. Instead, get out a set of crayons or colored markers and use those colors to express how your anger feels on the next page in your journal. Along with the colors, use shapes, lines, or other patterns to show what anger looks like to you.

As always, remember to think about everything you're feeling as you make your drawing. Anger should be the main emotion, but there will probably be others as well. Be aware of them. And always remember to seek help if you feel overwhelmed by your emotions.

1. As I was drawing my picture of anger, I felt the following emotions:

   When I go back and look at my picture, the strongest emotion I feel is _____ because…

2. I most quickly turn to food for comfort when I'm feeling…

   I eat the following foods to make my feelings of unease go away:

3. When the things I am feeling inside give me a sense that I'm losing control, I control my outward self by _____. This helps me to regain my sense of control and _____.

4. When I remember the pain I've felt in the past, my immediate reaction is to…

5. When I think about confronting _____ with my anger, it makes me want to…

I've been shielding _____ by not making him or her responsible for my pain because…

6. I feel a great deal of sadness over the loss of my _____ because…

If there were one thing I could reclaim that was lost in my past, it would be _____ because…

7. Take some time and write a "You hurt me because" letter to the person you feel is responsible for your pain. Tell that person how being hurt felt and what that pain has meant in your life. Use whatever language you want. This letter is not intended to actually be sent to the person. It's meant to help you verbalize what you've been trying to deny.

Dear _____,

You hurt me because…

It has been hard for me to express myself like this before because…

Anger Questionnaire

Recovering from an eating disorder requires relearning not only the proper response to food but also the proper response to anger. Anger occurs as a natural result of life. We get angry over large and small things every day. How we deal with anger is something we are taught, through either example or direct instruction. The training ground for dealing with anger is the family. Too often, we have learned inappropriate ways of dealing with our anger through the examples of our families. Consider your own upbringing on dealing with anger while responding to the following Anger Questionnaire:

1. Complete this sentence: Anger is _____.
2. What did you learn about anger as a child?
3. How did you express anger as a child?
4. Describe your most recent "anger" experience.
5. Describe the most angry moment in your entire life.
6. List the various ways in which you deal with anger.
7. What pleasure do you get from anger?
8. Do you have any positive way of getting rid of anger? If so, what is it?
9. How do you use anger as a weapon against others?
10. How do you use anger as a weapon against yourself?
11. What is your definition of anger?
12. What is your definition of hostility?
13. What is your definition of aggression?
14. How do you know when you are angry?
15. Where do you experience anger?
16. Complete this sentence: I feel angry when others _____.
17. Complete this sentence: I feel that my anger is _____.
18. Complete this sentence: When others express their anger, I feel _____.
19. Complete this sentence: I feel that the anger of others is _____.

IN THE RIGHT DIRECTION

LEARNING TO FEEL AGAIN

Anger and sadness—they've been with you so long you've probably convinced yourself that they aren't as bad as they seem. As you've worked through this chapter, it's likely that your numbness has suddenly fallen away and your anger and sadness have burst forth as smoldering rage and crushing despair. Your emotions haven't changed; you're just experiencing them without the dampening effect of your eating disorder.

Control over this anger and sadness has been the silent motivation behind your food addiction; but overeating, bingeing and purging, or starving your emotions into submission have only brought you a temporary respite from these emotions at a terrible physical and emotional cost.

The way to really control these emotions is first to acknowledge them as they really are. You need to understand them. You need to really *feel* them.

The person who hurt you took control over you, and he or she is still in control of you through your anger. It's time to make this person responsible for his or her actions, and it's time to take responsibility for your own future.

Freedom is a wonderful gift, but it's never cheap. Reexperiencing your anger and sadness in their fullness is the price you must pay to free yourself from their control. Confronting your anger and those who caused it will free you for the next step—forgiveness. Only then will you be able to start taking back the control over your emotions.

At the beginning, the emotions you reconnect with will seem overwhelmingly negative—anger and sadness...pain and shame. These have been building up behind your wall of denial, and when that wall is breached, those negative emotions are the ones that will come spilling out. After that initial flood, however, the emotional waters will calm and allow other feelings to bubble up to the surface. Joy, wonder, peace, gratitude. These emotions were once parts of your life and can be again, now that the logjam of your anger has been released. These positive, healing emotions will be of tremendous value to you on your road to recovery.

Consumed by your eating disorder, you have been trying to hold back toxic emotions. As these emotions are freed, you will be able to experience the ability the apostle Paul spoke about in Philippians 4:8: "Whatever is true, whatever is noble, whatever is right, whatever is pure, whatever is lovely, whatever is admirable—if anything is excellent or praiseworthy—think about such things."

And you'll receive the sheer gift from God—the realization that you are not only able to recognize these attributes around you, but also to recognize them in yourself.

AFFIRMING ACTION

God never said, "Don't be angry." Instead, he said, "In your anger do not sin" (Ephesians 4:26). Anger is a valid, sometimes reasonable, emotion. But God cautions us regarding this powerful emotion and warns us that anger must be dealt with carefully. Through the eating disorder, anger has been allowed to fester and cause great damage. Anger is powerful, yes, but God is more powerful. He is able to handle your anger—it is safe with him.

I am angry. I am hurt and in pain. It is so much I can't handle it alone.

Help me look at my anger, hurt to understand it. I have been angry for so long I'm afraid I won't know who I am without my anger. Reveal to me who I am, who I can be, without this consuming anger.

I will allow for joy.

Twelve

The Dance of Fear, Guilt, and Shame

Julie sat on the edge of her bed, paralyzed. Part of her wished for time to stop, for a pause in the constant pressure that was her life. So much was going on today, and she didn't know if she was going to make it.

"Just make it stop for a minute," she pleaded to no one and lay back on her neatly made bed, careful not to wrinkle her clothing. She closed her eyes and imagined herself in the midst of a great crowd of people. But the people had no faces, just movement. Each of them bumped against her, herding her here and there, without concern. There were simply too many of them, all pushing her to go in different directions. More people than she could count surrounded her, constantly moving, ever pressing.

Suddenly, Julie broke out in a cold sweat, her heart racing. With a gasp she opened her eyes and realized she'd dozed off. She wasn't getting enough sleep. She knew it, but there was nothing she could do about it. There just weren't enough hours in the day, so she regularly robbed from the night.

Besides, she didn't deserve to sleep at night if she couldn't get done what she needed to during the day. There was no one to blame but herself. Dragging herself off the bed, she sighed deeply and began gathering up her things. If she didn't get going she'd be late for history, and every tardy counted against her. Three tardies meant a reduction in grade point. A reduction in grade point would show up on her progress report, and she'd have to explain to her parents why her grades had "slipped." To avoid a scene with her parents, she'd have to do extra credit to make it up. Extra credit meant one more task to complete. One more thing to do before she could get some rest.

As she reached for the door to leave, Julie glanced at herself in the full-length mirror along the wall. Her hair was having its usual bad day, and no amount of concealer hid where her face had broken out. Her eyes were too close together, and the pants she wore made her hips look enormous.

She'd already decided she wasn't going to eat today. Maybe if she could go without eating for the next couple days, she could fit into that outfit her mother brought home for her. Every morning she'd hear, "When are you going to wear that outfit?" She wanted to yell, "When I don't look like a cow!" But that would get her a lecture on being "disrespectful," and, frankly, she didn't have the time.

If her mother was going to buy her something that made her look fat, she just wouldn't wear it until she was thin. Julie didn't deserve to wear it until she was thin. Then her mother couldn't say anything about it to her. Her father couldn't say anything about it to her. No one could.

DREADFUL COMPANIONS

Along with anger come companion emotions that need to be examined: fear, guilt, and shame. Anger can be an immediate response to pain in your life. Fear, guilt, and shame, however, follow close behind.

Fear

If you grew up in a rigid, perfectionistic family, you may have developed an intense fear of failure and rejection. If someone you desperately wanted approval from conditioned that approval on unrealistic goals of perfect behavior, you got the message that no matter how hard you tried, you were never good enough. If that person conditioned their approval on physical appearance, you got the message that being thin was the surest way to measure up.

It may be that your family stressed outward things, such as school performance, as the true measure of success, as opposed to inward considerations, such as how you were feeling. It may be that feelings were suppressed in your family or viewed as untrustworthy. Maybe you just didn't talk about them.

Your parents or other family members may still focus their attention on outward appearances. They may not be comfortable, even today, talking about feelings and emotions. They may express their approval only of your outward signs of success: your physical appearance, a prestigious job, exemplary school performance, a high salary, or material possessions. Success for them is determined by how you are "doing," as opposed to how you are feeling.

You need to recognize the possibility that your eating disorder has come about as a response to your need for this conditioned approval. If you were unable to gain acceptance in other areas of your life, you may have turned to your physical appearance as an avenue of acceptance. Your fear of rejection has metastasized into fear of being fat.

Guilt

Children are self-absorbed. They have yet to develop the maturity to think beyond themselves. And who can blame them? Children are inquisitive by nature, needy by circumstance, and cared for by design. From infancy, they have learned the effect they have on their world. Ask any parent what happens when a two-year-old discovers the power of saying no.

Children's frames of reference for sorting out the jumble of adult actions and motivations are their own experiences. So there is a tendency for children to blame themselves for family difficulties. A child whose parents are divorcing will ask himself what he did wrong. A child whose mother is angry all the time will wonder how she can make her mother happy. Children understand when something they have done wrong produces pain in others. An immature leap in logic can produce the false impression that when they experience pain themselves, they must be the cause of it. And those feelings lead to tremendous guilt.

Accepting the guilt for a situation can be easy for a child in another way. Children are adept at adaptation and surviving even the most dire circumstances. Their survival instincts and coping skills are formidable. By accepting the guilt for the pain in their lives, children seek to exert control over it. If they are responsible for the pain, they reason, they may have the power to alleviate it.

Eating disorders center anger, fear, and guilt on food. In order to control the anger, fear, and guilt, an anorexic will self-restrict food and liquids. A bulimic will binge to comfort the fear and purge out the guilt. An overeater will binge to bring comfort and settle for despair as a way to appease the guilt.

Shame

Eating disorders thrive in an atmosphere of shame. Without significant weakening in self-esteem and self-worth, the destructive behaviors of an eating disorder could not stand. In the progression of the eating disorder, shame over their inability to control their own behavior settles like a suffocating blanket over those with these disorders. The person who has learned to love and forgive herself would throw off that blanket. But to the person who has lived in an atmosphere of shame, that blanket is a familiar, acceptable place to hide.

The anorexic feels shame at never achieving impossible perfection. The bulimic and the overeater feel shame at the out-of-control bingeing. In addition, the bulimic who purges through vomiting or laxatives will feel shame at the very way the food is expelled from the body. The overeater feels shame at simply being fat. Eating disorders constantly attack self-esteem and promote self-doubt—the perfect breeding ground for shame.

Self-Hatred

Fear, guilt, and shame destroy peace, joy, and love. The eating disorder not only arises out of these negative feelings; it is perpetuated by them. An eating disorder whispers—sometimes screams—the following messages to the sufferer:

- "You're not good enough."
- "You're never going to be good enough."
- "You don't deserve to be loved."
- "You're responsible for what happens to you."
- "It's your fault."
- "You should do better."
- "You should look better."
- "There's something wrong with you."
- "You don't deserve to be happy."
- "No one will ever love you."

When these messages are repeated over and over, you believe them. You look around you and see ample proof of your imperfection, your weakness, your unlovable nature, your worthlessness. That dreary picture looks correct to you because you've seen it before.

CONSIDER THE SOURCE

For many of you, this dreary picture was painted in childhood by the very people who should have presented the world as a bright, vibrant, joyful explosion of life. But parents, being imperfect, can become so bogged down in their own darkness that they fail to realize they are dragging down their children with them. In order to heal from your eating disorder, you must take an honest look at the source of your negative messages and confront the real truth behind those messages.

If your parents are pressuring you to live a perfect life, they may not even be aware of the damage of this pressure. Your parents may be living vicariously through you, trying to force you to correct those areas of their lives that they were unable to master themselves. They may even have rationalized this pressure as a good thing, desiring to protect you, their child, "from making the same mistakes I did." In their desire to protect you from any mistake, it never dawned on them that you were suffocating.

For example, your parents may be pressuring you to achieve physical fitness as a shield against experiencing pain. Because fat means unhealthy. Unhealthy means illness. Illness means pain. Fat also means weak. Weak means vulnerable. Vulnerable means unprotected. Unprotected means pain.

Fat, in our society, also means lazy. Lazy means stupid. Stupid means substandard. There are parents who dread the thought of bringing up "substandard" children, for fear their own imperfections might be brought to light. The perfection of their children protects them from the scrutiny of others.

This pressure to be perfect, to succeed in order to protect your parents' image, might have revolved around food—thinness, having the "perfect" body—or it could have been goal-oriented. You may have felt forced to pursue certain education goals, job goals, marriage goals, money goals. When you did not meet these goals as your parents expected, you may have begun focusing on weight and body goals as a way of "making up" for your inability to conform to your parents' wishes in other areas.

Your eating disorder may also have had its roots in feelings of abandonment. This abandonment could have been physical—an actual withdrawal of a parent's presence—or it could have been emotional. If your father was emotionally distant, never mentally "there" with you, you may have felt abandoned even though he was physically present. This contradiction was probably confusing to you and might have led you to wonder if there was something inherently wrong with you that caused your father to think you were irrelevant.

You also may have experienced actual physical abandonment by one of your parents. If your parents divorced and your father left—and he didn't maintain close ties with you—then he abandoned you. He may even have remarried and started a "substitute" family, adding to your feelings of inadequacy.

The actual physical desertion of one parent may have been compounded by the emotional abandonment of the other. Following a divorce, the parent who raised you may have had little left over for you in the way of emotional nurturing. With nowhere else to turn, you sought your own companion/ solution. You chose food or thinness as a way to win back approval or attention or get back at the one who left you.

Feelings of abandonment often go hand-in-hand with guilt. When you were abandoned, somehow you felt responsible. This guilt over the devastation of your family and your anger over your inability to control what was happening in your life could have caused you to turn to self-destructive eating habits in order to cope. You were really trying to regain some semblance of control over an uncontrollable past.

Besides being abandoned, you may also have been abused as a child. When abuse is present, it increases the feelings of guilt and deals death blows to one's self-esteem. If someone was abusing you sexually, this person probably told you that what was happening was your fault, adding to your guilt. You probably concluded that you were being abused because you had been "bad" in some way. The abuse you suffered then, and the abuse you subject your body to now, may be justified in your own mind as atonement for the guilt you were made to feel over your abuse.

When you were growing up, you may have been told over and over, in a variety of ways, that you weren't good enough, smart enough, fast enough, thin enough, or just plain not enough of anything to please your parents. In order to numb this crushing sense of failure and the guilt it inspired, you began to control your anger by controlling your own body—how it was maturing and what you weighed. By concentrating on food, you learned how to temporarily drive out all painful thoughts.

Anger, fear, guilt, and shame may now be the only emotions you allow yourself to feel. These may be the only ones you're comfortable with because you don't feel worthy of the others. You don't permit yourself joy because you have too much to feel guilty about. You don't attempt love because you've been hurt too badly by rejection. You don't laugh because there isn't any room in your heart for delight.

The roots of your disorder go deep into your past. You need to allow that past to come to the surface so that you can look back at the experiences of your childhood, now that you are an adult, and begin to put your life into perspective. As a child, you couldn't understand what was happening to you. As an adult, you must. Only then can your healing go forward.

FOOD FOR THOUGHT

Rediscovering Childhood Through Adult Eyes

1. In my family, the thing I feared the most growing up was _____ because…

    My parents were happy when I…

    My parents disapproved of me when I…

2. These are the things that my parents put the most emphasis on when I was growing up:

    Even today my parents still want to talk about the following things:

    They still avoid talking about…

3. My mother's definition of success is:

    My father's definition of success is:

    To be successful for me means to be…

    I turned to my physical appearance as a way to gain acceptance because I couldn't…

    Things my mother wanted me to do that she was never able to do herself:

    Things my father wanted me to do that he was never able to do himself:

4. If my father abandoned me, either because he was gone
    or because he didn't seem to care, I wanted to…

    I'm still angry with my mother because, after my father left,
    she never…

    I felt guilty over being abandoned for the following reasons:

5. If I was abused, I blamed myself for the abuse because…

    When I was being abused, the person who abused me told me
    it was my fault for the following reasons:

    I believed what they said because…

6. When I was growing up, I thought the following things were
    wrong with me:

    I don't deserve to be happy because…

7. It's important that who you are now goes back and connects with
    the child you were, to help that child understand what happened.
    You must give that child the comfort you never received and pro-
    vide it with a sense of your protection. That child still remains
    inside you. Until you can give it what it needs, your inner child
    will thwart the journey toward healing. The child inside is pleading
    with you not to abandon it on your way to health.

    If you have a doll or stuffed animal, especially one from your child-
    hood, get it. If you don't, you might want to consider buying one,
    maybe even one that you've seen as an adult and wished you could
    have had as a child. Borrow one from a friend if you have to or use
    one of your own children's toys. Whichever one you chose, make
    sure you feel a connection to it.

8. Hold that doll or stuffed animal. Hug it close. Give it all the comfort and love you never received. Stroke it, brush its hair, and sing to it, if that's what you feel like doing. Make that doll the child within you.

Tell your doll all the words of affirmation and acceptance you so desperately wanted to hear while you were growing up.

Hold your doll and tell yourself (as if it were you as a child) that it wasn't your fault you were left by someone you loved. Remind your doll that you're here now and you're not going to leave. Tell yourself it wasn't your fault you were abused. Comfort yourself through your doll for the terrible pain you felt at being abused.

Keep your doll near to remind you of the child within. As you go through the rest of this book, go back and comfort your doll whenever you feel the need to. Put it where you can see it.

For right now, funnel your feelings through the doll. Later, you'll be able to see it for what it is—a doll—and learn to give those feelings of love and comfort directly to yourself.

IN THE RIGHT DIRECTION

FACING THE CHAOS WITHIN

The lawn is cut and edged. The hedges are trimmed, flower beds weeded. The exterior of the house is freshly painted. This is a neat and tidy place, immaculate in presentation. You'd never guess that chaos resides behind that perfect exterior.

Inside is a jumble of objects, strewn from room to room, dropped, abandoned, neglected. The owner of the house lives inside with all the clutter.

Others may not be permitted past the front door, but the owner knows the truth. The owner lives with the dichotomy of the hidden and the visible.

For a long time, you've been living in a house where the only thing that mattered was your outside. Your energy and time have been devoted to its perfect presentation, to the detriment of the inner spaces where you really live. Anger, fear, and guilt have been allowed to set up housekeeping while you were busy making sure your stomach didn't bulge and your breasts and hips were flat. Room by room, these negative emotions have taken over your house.

Somewhere, hidden away in a corner, frightened of all the horrible sounds of chaos, is a lonely, hurting child, a child who longs to be rescued from the terror that never seems to stay away.

This child is waiting for you to come and make sense of the chaos.

The first step is awareness: when you look around and understand that it makes no sense to have a trimmed outside when your inside is in shambles.

The second step is acceptance: when you admit the shambles of your life and give up trying to prove that it's only the outside that counts.

The third step is acknowledgment: when you acknowledge that God alone has the power to help you overcome your eating disorder and put your life back together.

The rest of the journey is assurance: when you accept that God loves and values you.

Affirming Action

First John 4:18 says, "There is no fear in love. But perfect love drives out fear." A perfectionist reads this verse and says to himself, "Then I'll always fear, because I can never have perfect love for God. I deserve fear. I don't deserve to be loved."

But the perfect love spoken of is God's love for you, not your love for God. You do not need to be perfect in love; God already is. And it is his perfect love for you that drives out fear, removes guilt, and rescues from shame.

Focus your thoughts on God's perfection and be released from the need to be perfect yourself.

Focus your thoughts on God's love and be released from the fear of his wrath.

Focus your thoughts on God's forgiveness and be released from the bondage of guilt.

Focus your thoughts on God's acceptance and be released from the shroud of shame.

God, help me give up my need for perfection. I feel so afraid; comfort me with your love. I feel such guilt; refresh me with your forgiveness. I feel so ashamed; show me my worth. Help me to love myself.

Kirsten's Story

When it feels like all hope is lost, when all your energy to fight is gone, remember to let God carry your burdens. The Lord can bring hope to the hopeless, light to the darkness, and energy to the lifeless.

I was there in that empty place. The darkness had invaded every ounce of my soul. I quit fighting. I was ready to die. There was so much missing from my life, and it seemed that each step I took toward the eating disorder was a step farther from reality. I no longer had the desire to work, be social, be married, or be alive. I had so much to be thankful for, yet I was lonely and hopeless.

And that is when God reached out to me. He brought caring, experienced counselors into my life—people who provided hope when I couldn't find it on my own. I became so desperately hopeless that I allowed others into my secret, shameful world.

I learned to look at recovery as a process. I addressed the many different areas that needed healing. I also learned to accept that the process was going to be intense, and I learned just how important it was that I face each component of recovery with determination and dedication.

Recovery from an eating disorder has very little to do with food. Yes, you can control food and get things in order for a while. But until you look at the root causes, the eating disorder will always be under the surface ready to grow again. I learned to dig out the roots. It has been the most challenging and rewarding work I have ever done. Temporary fixes no longer worked. Facing the roots was my only hope.

Food does not control me the way it used to. I still find myself turning back to food in times of trouble, but I have discovered that it doesn't provide relief for me anymore. The key for me was to learn to enjoy food again. In the past, food was either my friend or my worst enemy. Now it is neither. Food is a source of energy, and enjoying the variety of foods and how they are prepared has been part of the process of recovery for me.

Recovery has taught me to embrace the people I love. I no longer isolate and push people away. Food was my friend. Food replaced the need to have intimate relationships with people. Food accepted me, loved me, and destroyed me! By walking away from food, I was able to run into the arms of caring people. God put wonderful people in my life to help me when I needed them the most.

I finally understood that, though the most important component of my recovery was my faith in God, there were other areas that had to be dealt with before the despair could be lifted. God's work in my life taught me that I am unique and special. God has a purpose for my life, and recovery is the beginning of discovering that purpose. I have learned I am not alone. I have family and friends who love and support me. I have counselors to depend on. I also have other people who understand what I am going through because they have battled an eating disorder. God places people in our lives who can help us develop a greater understanding of ourselves. The only obstacle in the way of my recovery was me!

I am not living each day for food, and I do not let food determine my mood. Peace has taken on a whole new meaning to me, and I am grateful to have discovered how to separate my body size and weight from my overall sense of well-being.

I pray that these words will provide you with comfort, hope, and the desire to walk down the road to recovery. It is difficult, but the rewards are endless!

—Kirsten

Thirteen

Healing As a Journey

Maybe this wasn't such a great idea, Janice thought. She was in mile two of a five-mile run, and it wasn't going well. Her legs hurt, she was breathing hard, and up ahead lay the steepest hill of the route.

I could just turn around right now and go back, she told herself. *I'd still have put in several miles. That would be okay.* But it didn't feel okay. Janice had really wanted to complete this run.

Just keep going as long as you can. If you just can't make it, you can stop.

With that decision made, she felt herself relax into the rhythm of her pace. Then she began to feel the incline of the hill. Looking up, all she saw was a steep grade.

"Don't look up," she said quietly. *Just don't look up. Keep your eyes forward. You can do this.* Her breath was a steady stream of in and out, in and out, deep and quickened. Her calf muscles protested the angle of the climb.

You could stop now, she reminded herself, as she strained a third of the way up the hill. *No one would care if you just stopped and walked the rest of the way up.* But that didn't feel right, either. She would care. She'd promised herself to keep going as long as she could, and even though it was difficult, Janice knew she could go on.

She adjusted the swing of her arms to assist her stride. *It won't be much longer now,* she promised her lungs and her legs. She was two-thirds of the way up the hill. She wasn't going very fast, but she was moving forward.

Once I reach the top of the hill, it's a gradual decline for about half a mile. I can stretch out then and recover a bit.

Just a little bit more.

As she neared the top of the hill, Janice rewarded herself by lifting up her eyes. She didn't think she could breathe any harder or run any faster, but the crest of the hill was in sight. *Just a little more… Just a little bit more…*

And then she was at the top. The road evened out, and Janice could see the gentle downward slope ahead. *I did it! I didn't give up!* She smiled, astonished. Her breathing evened out as she ran down the hill, stretching out the muscles in her legs.

Janice felt great. She hadn't given up. She hadn't stopped. She was still running and oh-so-grateful for this patch of easier road. It would help her get ready for the next hill.

Janice realized she was proud of herself. That hill had been difficult, but she hadn't given up. Instead, she'd found the strength to keep going.

TAKING A BREATHER

The previous chapters have dealt with—and dredged up—some pretty serious emotions. At this point, you may be wondering about the wisdom of even having started this book! That's all right. What you are remembering and reexperiencing is painful and unpleasant. In the Introduction, I cautioned that there might be times like this.

The healing journey is not without hills and valleys. You may feel as if you've climbed a vertical hill. Take a breather. While you don't want to stop altogether, it's not a bad time to coast a little bit and reflect on what you've accomplished so far.

The journey you are on involves a process, and it requires time. True healing doesn't happen overnight and isn't accomplished through a single blinding light of insight. Although "light bulb" revelations can occur during your journey, "light bulb" healing does not. There is no magic formula that takes you from "sick one minute" to "cured the next."

You've started looking at those people in your past who have hurt you in some way. As you've relived childhood pain and abuse, you've begun to overcome your denial and bring some real understanding to what happened to you back then. You've realized that you're older now, you're not a frightened child anymore, and that it's okay to reveal the "secrets" of the past. There's no need to protect your family or an abuser any longer. You've looked outward, and you're beginning to look inward as well.

A New Perspective

Your eating disorder started as a coping mechanism for dealing with an often chaotic and confusing world. It became your way of coping with anger. You're starting to really relive that anger now.

Your next step is to find a new perspective with which to view your past. If you were to hit your thumb with a hammer, your initial reaction would be anger. You'd be furious with the hammer for hitting your thumb, and you'd be mad at yourself for not being more careful. After the initial rush of pain was over, you'd realize that the hammer wasn't to blame; it's just a tool. You're not to blame either: Hitting your thumb was an accident. Once you realize this, you've put what happened into its proper perspective.

Up until now, you've been looking back at the events of the past and seeing them through the eyes of a child. As an adult, you know that children, especially those of past generations, were not often told all the reasons behind the decisions made concerning them. Your parents may have felt it was too much of a burden on you to explain certain family circumstances, especially difficult ones.

As a child, not being privy to all the reasons why things happened or why things were said, you filled in those blanks with your own explanations, using the full imagination of your childhood. This can result in faulty conclusions. Somewhere along the line you may have concluded that all the distressing events around you were your fault. By reliving these events and looking at them from an older, more mature perspective, you have the opportunity to correct your faulty childhood conclusions and adopt a more well-rounded understanding of what happened and why.

On the other hand, the unfairness of pain and hurt can be a bitter pill to swallow, especially if the ones who hurt you were family members. Once you realize you are not to blame for the circumstances of your past, you might find yourself asking, *How could they have done that to me? Didn't they know how much they hurt me?*

Parents aren't perfect. They are people, capable of mistakes and failure, and these mistakes may result in their children's pain. They simply may not have been attuned to how their actions and attitudes were affecting you. It is not an excuse, but it is an explanation. Sometimes an explanation will have to suffice, except in the case of flagrant abuse.

Some of you will have been neglected, dismissed, pressured, driven, silenced. Others of you will have been sexually abused, physically beaten, or deliberately abandoned. Pain, however, is still pain no matter how it is inflicted. As you reflect on how you have been hurt, an obvious question will come to mind: Should the person who hurt you have known better? In some cases—especially those involving flagrant abuse—the answer is yes. The parent or the one who hurt or abused you may have been carrying on faulty parenting skills they learned as children. They may also have been abused. Or it may be that you were a victim of a truly evil person who needed no reason beyond their own hellish nature. If some abuse can never be justified, it can, however, be understood. In most cases, there will be a "why" to help explain the past.

In cases other than flagrant abuse, should the person who hurt you have known better? The answer is "probably." People generally know when they are hurting another person. They know when they answer in anger or respond selfishly or are cruel and sarcastic. They may know when they do these things but explain them away because of fatigue or frustration. Some parents can have a difficult time asking forgiveness from their children. It upsets what they see as the hierarchy of the family. Some parents would rather hide behind the cloak of parental authority than admit how they have injured their own children.

Do not let the question of "Shouldn't they have known better?" stall your journey. Your answer may differ from theirs. The person who hurt you may continue to reject any responsibility for their actions. You may never hear an admission and an apology. The person who hurt you may have specific, definitive reasons for their inability to understand the ramifications of their actions. The person may have truly been unaware of how much you were hurting.

You must move on. The healing journey requires you to turn your focus away from others and onto yourself. Once you have uncovered the pain in your past, it will be tempting to stay there, focusing on the mistakes of others and blaming them for all your misery. In order to heal, you must turn inward and take a hard look at your own responsibility for the choices you've made. Others may have been responsible for your past, but only you are responsible for your future.

You must *want* to get well. Once you have understood that something is drastically wrong with the choices you are making in your life, the responsibility for making positive change lies solely with you. You must replace the false control of the eating disorder with a positive control based on your new understanding of yourself and your past.

Please don't give up on the journey because the path isn't always easy and level. Neither is *life*.

FOOD FOR THOUGHT

Mapping Your Progress

1. Imagine your healing process—and your work through this book—as a journey. Draw a map in your journal or notebook of your progress so far. Show the path you've taken, the obstacles you've had to overcome or work around, the high points where you've come to understand a hidden truth. Label it "My Journey."

Remember, don't worry about the quality of your drawing. Use color and whatever details help cement how you're really feeling. This picture is for you, a visual chronicle of the work you've done so far.

2. Go back through your journal to refresh your memory. Read over the statements and questions you've already answered. Look at the pictures and the collages you've made. Take a moment to put this journey into perspective.

   Fill in your journey up to this point and then, if you like, anticipate some of the highs and lows that may come up as you continue. If you can anticipate the lows, it may help you to get through them. You'll have an idea they are coming, although you may not be sure exactly when.

3. Looking at your map, what are the major high points so far? What are the major valleys so far?

4. As you look over your past, what are you able to see now, from a more mature viewpoint, that you haven't been able to see before?

   Think about letting go of your anger. What are your immediate reactions?

   Read these next statements aloud and then write down your answers.

   I've always thought I was at fault for what happened to me. Now I can see that what happened to me happened because…

   It's difficult to forgive my parents for not being perfect because…

   The way people parent today is different from when I grew up in the following ways:

5. Read over the following and respond as honestly as you can.

It's hard for me to accept responsibility for my eating disorder because...

I realize I've contributed to my eating disorder by...

In order to get well, I've been able to...

I choose to accept the responsibility for my future because...

6. You have to want to get well. You have to believe you can get well. Use the following statements to reinforce your desire and your belief in your own healing.

I have the following reasons for wanting to get well:

These are the reasons I know I can get well:

IN THE RIGHT DIRECTION

SHIFTING FOCUS

This chapter has been a place for you to pause and get your bearings. You've been experiencing waves of emotions that have tossed and turned you about. It's time for some calmer waters.

Everything we do, see, and experience is sifted through the filter of our perspective. It provides the lens through which we see the world. The last few chapters have helped you focus on the perspective of your childhood, which is essential. The child you were then helps explain who you are today. But the person you are today is more than the child you were then. As you begin to understand your world from the perspective of your childhood self, you need to shift toward a view of who you are now.

Shifting your viewpoint results in understanding. So much of what happened to you was beyond your ability to grasp. Unable to obtain reasons you could understand, you came up with incomplete explanations of your own. Your childhood explanations led to anger, fear, and shame, which led to your eating disorder.

This process of shifting perspective should be like tumblers clicking into place on a combination lock. As you turn toward a greater understanding, each tumbler should fall into its proper position, allowing you to unlock the pain of your past and open the door on a new understanding and appreciation of who you are today. This is a time to remember where you are now and how you got there—and to remind yourself of where you're going.

Affirming Action

Gary Smalley, in his book *The Amazing Connection Between Food and Love*, includes a wonderful list called "Seven Principles to Lifelong Victory." In parentheses, I've added the emphasis I think is valuable for you at this point in your journey.

1. Identify your problem areas. *(Identify your pain.)*
2. Admit your inadequacy. *(Admit your eating disorder.)*
3. Cry out to God. *(Give your eating disorder and your pain to God.)*
4. Believe that God will rescue you. *(Allow yourself to hope again.)*
5. Be willing to wait as long as it takes. *(Allow God to do his part and commit to doing yours.)*
6. Expect God to give you a breakthrough. *(Give up your self-hate.)*
7. Pray faithfully and persistently. *(Submit control of your future to God.)*[1]

I want you to strengthen your resolve to stay the course to healing. You've been asked to look at the truth about others and yourself. You've been asked to begin the process of releasing the harmful effects of the past. Decide again to be healthy—emotionally, physically, relationally, spiritually. Resolve to live in freedom, not in bondage to an eating disorder. Allow God to love you. And, through him, relearn how to love yourself.

God, thank you for strength and patience. Help me not to give up. Thank you for giving me patience and hope.

Fourteen

Finding the Way
to Forgiveness

Drew sat in his car for a minute, looking out at the same white shutters, the same juniper bushes taking over the sidewalk. The years hadn't been particularly kind to the house. It seemed tired, neglected. Drew's mother had always been the one to keep the flowerbeds up and badger his father to put a new coat of paint on the house.

They'd divorced when Drew was in college, seeing no reason to keep up the charade—not that they'd been very effective at it by the time he hit high school. His mother had left then, gone to Dubuque, Ohio, to live near her sister. After that, nothing seemed to get done anymore to the house or yard. Now Drew was forty-three years old—a grown man who was almost afraid to walk up those steps and go inside his childhood home.

Inside, his father waited. Inside, everything probably still looked the same. Same couches, same chairs, same dishes, same bed. Oh, the television had been different two Christmases ago. It was bigger.

He'd called his father just before Halloween and said he was coming to see him. "Don't worry," Drew told him over the phone, "I'll stay at the motel down the road. I don't want to put you out. I just want to see you." *That's not exactly true,* he admitted to himself, trying to make out any sort of movement behind the half-drawn drapes. *I don't know that I want to see you as much as I need to see you.*

Taking a deep breath, Drew opened the car door and climbed out, careful to lock it. The neighborhood had really gone downhill over the past few years.

I wonder if he'll make me ring the bell, he thought, as he glanced both ways and crossed the street. *It'd be just like him to watch me the whole way and make me wait at the front door like a salesman.* Bitterness threatened to overwhelm him for a moment, but Drew fought it back down. *That's not gonna help. That's not what I'm here for.*

A moment after he rang the bell, the front door opened. His father said, "Hi," and moved aside to let him in. The house smelled different, wrong. It smelled musty. *He's getting old,* Drew thought.

His dad asked about his flight and what kind of car he'd rented. Drew let him steer the conversation around meaningless things as he worked up the courage to say what he needed to say. *God, this is going to be hard.* Sensing that Drew was about to say something, his father hesitated, letting the stream of conversation putter to a stop.

"Dad," Drew began, "I... I, ahh..." He got up and went over to the window. Even in the middle of the afternoon the house was dim. His father waited silently.

"I've been doing a lot of thinking, Dad," he finally said, quietly. "It's been hard for me to be around you because of all the stuff growing up. But I'd like that to be different. I want you to know I've forgiven you." *There, I've said it. I can't take it back. The ball's in your court, Dad. But I've already won the game.*

NAVIGATING THE ROAD TO FORGIVENESS

Forgiveness is a major destination on your healing journey. If the child of the past and the adult of the present are to integrate fully into the healed person of the future, there comes a time to release the hurts of the past, to forgive. The road that lies beyond is one of recovery and health. Forgiveness builds a solid foundation so you can grow beyond the hurt and pain fueling your anger and your eating disorder. You take control over your pain through the act of forgiveness instead of through the actions of your eating disorder.

Forgiveness doesn't mean you forget what was done to you, but that you forgive those responsible, whether they deserve your forgiveness or not. "Forgive and forget" is simply not the way our brains work. As humans, we will always remember. Sometimes the memories, especially the painful ones, will be vivid. But forgiveness allows us to set ourselves free from the negative effects of remembered pain. Forgiveness dilutes the power these memories have in the present and allows us to define ourselves as who we are now, not by the pain in our past.

Roadblocks to Recovery

Anger, fear, shame, and guilt—the debilitating emotions you've been feeling—get in the way of being able to experience forgiveness. These emotions have been your companions up to now. They will not want to be left behind.

You've already gone a long way toward placing the responsibility for your pain on those who deserve it. Doing that is healthy, but beware of anger. As you come to acknowledge the truth about the pain you've been feeling, you will reexperience the anger you've been suppressing through your eating disorder. This anger is familiar, but without the confines of the eating disorder, it may seem overwhelming. The danger is to want to remain angry, wallowing in placing blame, which only leads to more anger. It takes great courage to confront those who hurt you, to acknowledge the power they have to cause you pain, and to make a conscious choice, for your health and well-being, to forgive them and move on.

Resentment at finally understanding what happened to you may foster an intense desire to retaliate against those who caused your pain. You must fight against remaining in a blaming mode. Instead, you need to move beyond blame and toward forgiveness. Forgiveness is the balm that allows your soul to heal and you to grow beyond your pain and anger.

It is also possible that you have an unnatural fear of conflict in any form. You may fear being rejected again by the person who hurt you. It may be easier to continue to take out your resentment on yourself rather than to express the truth to that person openly. Your well-established pattern of the addiction can seem much more comfortable and safe than the unknown consequences of dealing with the person who hurt you and extending that person forgiveness.

Acknowledging your truth and laying blame where it belongs will surely cause conflict between you and the person who has hurt you. Expressing forgiveness, however, allows for a safer avenue of communication. Those responsible for your pain may have no idea you feel the way you do. When you can approach them from an attitude of forgiveness, you provide them with a buffer to cushion the blow of old images shattered and the realization of their own mistakes and responsibility.

Finding out about your past is important for understanding the relevance of that past for your life in the present. As you work to overcome anger and fear, you will also need to work to overcome your own feelings of shame and guilt. The best way to overcome these roadblocks is to forgive yourself for your responsibility in your eating disorder. If you can find the strength to forgive others, it will be easier to forgive yourself for the choices you have made.

Remember, though, that you cannot control anyone's response but your own. Whether or not the people in your life accept your forgiveness, you need to be sure in your own mind that there is something to forgive. Trust yourself and your memories. In every relationship, there are hurtful places that need the healing of forgiveness. Perhaps you will need to start by working through smaller hurts and then work toward acknowledgment of larger ones, within the framework of forgiveness.

Showing forgiveness, even to the person who admits no need for it, allows you to show a healing example of what love and acceptance are all about. If you did not receive love and acceptance from the ones who hurt you, or if they were deficient in their ability to love you, you can give love and forgiveness to those persons as precious gifts. In this way, you can break the cycle of an unloving response.

Forgiveness means letting go and getting on with life. Forgiveness puts an end to anger and its ability to control behavior. It leads to restored relationships with those you love. Even if such a relationship is not yet possible—

because your loved ones refuse to accept responsibility for the pain they caused you—you have done your part. Knowing that you have done all you can to mend the relationship brings its own sense of peace.

Roadblocks to Forgiveness

Forgiving someone is never easy. It does not happen overnight; it is a process. Often it requires getting over the faulty beliefs and practices taught to you by the very people you are trying to forgive.

Beware the need to punish. In your anger, you may withhold the healing act of forgiveness as a way to punish or to retaliate against the person who hurt you.

Beware the desire to continue focusing on yourself. Forgiveness allows for you to move on to a healthier focus on life, away from your self-consuming eating disorder and on to a healthy balance of focuses and interests.

Beware the belief that you deserve to be hurt and miserable. You don't; that's your eating disorder talking to you. Forgiveness will bring you peace, healing, and relief.

Beware of pride. Your eating disorder has brought you a perverted sense of pride as a way to counteract the pain. Forgiveness, by lessening the pain, interferes with the maintenance of that pride.

If you were never provided with examples of love and forgiveness growing up in your immediate family, where can you get them? Try to remember the people who did give them to you as a child, maybe a grandparent or a family friend. Then think back to how much you needed love growing up. Remember how you would have felt if you had received acceptance. As a forgiving adult, you can give those who wronged you the very things you were denied as a child, breaking the circle of abuse.

If you have constructed the myth of a happy childhood, giving up that dream will be painful. You will have to discard your idea of the perfect mom and dad or the image of an idyllic, loving family. Instead, you can establish a new relationship with your family, just as they are.

For some people, their pain and hurt are so deep inside of them that their ability to forgive is buried under layers of anger and resentment. If this description fits you, you will need to search outside of yourself for the strength to forgive. Again, you need to understand that forgiveness is something you can rarely accomplish immediately. You've lived with your pain for many years; allow yourself the time you need to work through your need to forgive.

Your eating disorder is a response to your pain and anger. If you can understand what happened, get past the anger, and forgive the pain, the reason for your behavior will no longer exist. When the reason no longer exists, and the health-related complications of your behavior are addressed, true healing becomes a reality.

The Joys of Forgiveness

- Forgiveness allows you to reclaim your personal happiness and find release from bondage to debilitating emotions.
- Forgiveness allows you to reclaim intimacy in your relationships by giving you closure over the painful ones so you can truly enjoy the healing ones.
- Forgiveness allows you to seek out appropriate forms of comfort.
- Forgiveness allows you to truly throw out those harmful emotions instead of storing and recycling them.
- Forgiveness allows you to refresh your mind by improving your self-esteem and realizing the awesome ability to forgive that lies within you.
- Forgiveness allows you the freedom to seek your true potential unencumbered by your eating disorder.
- Forgiveness allows you to amplify your strengths and gifts over your weaknesses.

Proactive Forgiveness

Once you have acknowledged the truth of your pain, you must decide to forgive. You have just read the incredible benefits of doing so. But what if you're just not there yet? What if you understand all the pluses but still don't feel like forgiving? The first step is to state your truth aloud, even if it's only to yourself. Put into words how you are feeling and what has been done to you. Saying the words aloud is a way to let them go.

Next, decide to forgive—not because you want to, not because it feels good, and not because it's deserved, but because it is the healing thing for you to do. A conscious choice on your part to forgive can counteract your conscious decision to continue in the behaviors of your eating disorder. Your will is the same, but you are choosing to use it in a healthy, uplifting way.

As you work through what your forgiveness should look like, realize you may need outside guidance. This will be especially true if you have been abused in some way. It simply may not be advisable to confront or communicate with an abusive person. Your forgiveness may need to be within you, or through a remote method, in order to protect you from further injury. Seek help from a professional counselor or trained pastor. Friends are wonderful resources, but you should look to someone trained in these issues whenever possible.

Learn all you can. Please consider reading more on this topic. The more sound information you have, the more you will gain a realization that healing is possible. At the end of the book is a resource section with many valuable materials for you to consider.

FOOD FOR THOUGHT

Learning to Forgive

1. In chapter 11, you wrote a "You hurt me because" letter to someone in your life. Go back and reread that letter.

In that same chapter, you also drew a picture of what anger looked like to you. Go back and look at that picture. Remember what you were feeling when you wrote that letter and drew that picture. Was it pleasant? Did it make you feel good? Now, in the next two steps, you're going to draw a different sort of picture and write a different kind of letter.

2. Draw what forgiveness looks like with crayons or markers, or paste in representative pictures from your magazines. This may be hard. You've lived with anger for a long time. It is more familiar to you. You may need to remember how you felt when someone forgave you and what that forgiveness meant to you. Express how that feels in your drawing.

3. After drawing a picture of forgiveness, write another letter to the same person you wrote to before. Again, this is not an actual letter to send but a way for you to verbalize in a safe way the forgiveness you need to extend. Instead of a "You hurt me because" letter, which emphasizes the action of the other person, write an "I forgive you because" letter, which will emphasize the control you are taking back for yourself. You are no longer the object of the action but the initiator of it.

4. When I looked back at my picture of anger, I reexperienced feelings of…

    As I was drawing my picture of forgiveness, I felt…

5. As I look back, I realize I've been living in a world of anger, and it makes me feel…

6. When I think about forgiving the person who hurt me, it makes me feel…

My letter expressing my _____ was easier for me to write because…

7. It seems as if all my life I've been trying to say those things to my _____, but I was always afraid to because…

8. The following people or events have helped me better understand what forgiveness is all about:

9. Think back to the story at the beginning of this chapter. How did it make you feel? If you could have the ideal situation to bestow forgiveness on someone who needs your forgiveness the most, what would that situation look like? Where would it take place? Who would you forgive? What would you say?

IN THE RIGHT DIRECTION

THE PROCESS OF FORGIVENESS

Forgiveness isn't an act; it's a process. Someone bumps you in the elevator and says, "Oh, I'm sorry." "Oh, that's all right," you say. You've forgiven that person. But on a subconscious level, you looked at that person and judged the reason why they bumped you and the manner in which they apologized before you assured them, "Oh, that's all right." Even though the time from their bump to your acceptance of their apology was very short, your forgiveness was still a process that took into account a variety of factors, not the least of which was how you were feeling that day. If such a small event requires evaluation, think what the process must look like when applied to the incidents of abuse and pain in your past.

Start with prayer. Forgiveness is a tall order, and the power and strength needed to forgive are formidable. But remember that nothing is impossible with God. He is able to give you the ability to extend forgiveness. He is, in fact, an expert at forgiveness: He extends it to us all the time.

While I firmly believe that forgiveness is vital to a successful journey toward healing, don't pile additional burdens onto yourself if you are unable to give instant forgiveness to yourself or to those who are responsible for your pain. This isn't a bump on an elevator. The process of your forgiveness requires time, perspective, and patience.

No matter how hard you've tried to suppress your anger, it's very near the surface. Any chink in your armor, and it comes exploding outward. Forgiveness is deeper down, harder to get to. You'll have to dig for it, like any real treasure.

And while you are working toward this gem of forgiveness, place your wounded heart in God's hands for safekeeping. Allow him to provide you comfort and safety. At the start of each day, deliberately turn to God and not to your behavior with food.

AFFIRMING ACTION

As you are working toward forgiveness, cultivate gratefulness. A grateful heart is insulation for future hurts. Gratefulness allows you to focus on the good things happening in your life. It allows you to respond positively to the gifts God bestows on all of us every day. By developing an attitude of gratitude, forgiveness becomes easier. When it is put into the context of all the wonderful, valuable things in your life for which you are grateful, forgiveness will come more easily.

God, thank you for loving and forgiving me. Help my personal happiness to grow each day as I trust you. Empower me to extend forgiveness, even when it is difficult. Help me to say each day that I am a grateful and loving person. Help me to say each day that I am a forgiving person. Grant me your peace.

Fifteen

The Perfect Father

The church parking lot was filling up when Pamela drove in. Pulling into a space away from the main building, she made her way across the asphalt to the side entrance. She ducked inside and walked down the back stairs to the basement, to the "education wing," as it was called. Every Sunday morning, Pamela volunteered to work with the five-year-olds. She'd been cornered by the children's ministry director almost a year ago, and it had been easier to just say yes.

She had to admit, though, that now she looked forward to working with the little kids. Just being at church made her feel closer to God. She felt less like an intruder because she had a ministry to do. She was comfortable with the basement and the brightly painted classroom. Sometimes, she couldn't bring herself to go upstairs to the main auditorium.

Megan was already in the classroom, getting things ready for the kids, when Pamela arrived and hung up her coat on the rainbow-colored pegs by the door. Megan was the teacher of the class, and Pamela was her helper. Megan was there every Sunday; sometimes Pamela just didn't feel good enough to come to church.

They exchanged some small talk, but, luckily, the kids soon came piling into the classroom, and all the focus was on them. Pamela felt uncomfortable when she was the focus of anything.

Megan sat in the front of the class, with the children seated on the carpet. Pamela's job was to sit at the back of the class and help out if anyone needed to go to the bathroom, and to make sure no one squirmed too much or started bothering a neighbor. It was a pretty simple job—just keep stating the rules, which she did in soft, firm tones.

On this Sunday, Megan was talking about God. But instead of telling them who God is, she was asking them to tell her who God is for them. Some of their answers were so precious, Pamela had to smile.

"I like God," Justin said loudly, after raising his hand all the way up to the ceiling and barely waiting to be called on by Miss Megan. "God is like my daddy." Justin's father was a large, soft-spoken man who always smiled and gave Justin a big hug every time he picked him up from class. Without warning, tears sprang to Pamela's eyes.

With unexpected clarity, Pamela realized she didn't like God. She believed in God. She feared God. She was in awe of God. But she couldn't honestly say she liked him. She thought of God like her own father—stern, strict, unapproachable. How could she feel God truly loved her with all of the things she kept hidden in her life?

Composing herself quickly, she brushed the tears off her face and started singing with the children, "Jesus loves me, this I know, for the Bible tells me so..."

YOUR SPIRITUAL CONNECTION

In the journey toward healing so far, I have encouraged you to take a realistic look at yourself and others. The whole-person approach also encourages individuals to take a good look at their spiritual connections. I believe it is vital for you to establish, regain, or strengthen a healthy relationship with God. I believe we are spiritual beings. An acceptance of that fact can greatly aid your recovery.

Spiritual Disconnects

Over the years, I have worked with many people who have various reasons why they feel disconnected from God. Their reasons depend upon their spiritual circumstances. If you also feel disconnected, perhaps you will see yourself somewhere in the following.

I don't believe in God. Some people have never developed a faith in God. For most, it is not that they have rejected God but that they have not been exposed to God while growing up. God is simply not a part of life. I have seen many people come to faith through their struggle with their eating disorder. When faced with an overwhelming addiction, people find great comfort in learning about a God who cares. "'But I will restore you to health and heal your wounds,' declares the LORD" (Jeremiah 30:17).

I didn't know I could have a relationship with God. Some people have a faith in God but have no idea that a relationship with him is possible or permissible. God exists as a fact of the universe, like the solar system, but without any connection with us as people. I have seen great joy when people realize they can exchange their relationship with food for a truly satisfying relationship with God. "The LORD is near to all who call on him, to all who call on him in truth" (Psalm 145:18).

I had a relationship with God, and I still have an eating disorder. Many people I work with come from a background of religious faith. They believed in God while growing up but have assumed, because of their eating disorder, that their faith has been rendered ineffective. This false assumption is one we work very hard to overturn because it is faith, however disconnected, that will be their greatest asset in overcoming their eating disorders. Faith, even incomplete faith, is very powerful, as one man declares in Mark 9:24: "I do believe; help me overcome my unbelief!"

I've failed God, and he is displeased with me. Shame and guilt whisper this message to so many with an eating disorder. Because they assume God has written them off, they find it very tempting to write themselves off. This apathetic, destructive approach works against any desire to keep trying, to keep hoping. Perhaps the greatest argument against this false assumption is the message of John 3:16: "For God so loved the world that he gave his one and only Son, that whoever believes in him shall not perish but have eternal life."

I am angry at God. The anger that fuels an eating disorder does not always stay within the confines of the individual. I have worked with people who are furious with God for the pain that has happened in their lives. They resist surrendering their will to him because they don't believe he can be trusted. In other words, if he truly loved them, why were they hurt and why do they suffer with this eating disorder? These are significant questions that are answered as people begin to acknowledge their pain and correctly assess who or what is truly responsible. The reason for their anger is understandable; the object of their anger, God, is not. Together, we work to gain an understanding of Psalm 4:4-5: "In your anger do not sin; when you are on your beds, search your hearts and be silent. Offer right sacrifices and trust in the LORD."

I am afraid of God. This spiritual disconnect can be very strong for those who grew up in a strict, rigid, religious household. God was presented as a punisher, as a wrathful God to be approached only in fear and trembling. It is one of the great joys of my life and work to be able to present God as he truly is: a loving, caring Father who is slow to anger. Even Moses in the Old Testament, who was witness to God in his most awesome power, was inspired to describe God as "the LORD, the compassionate and gracious God, slow to anger, abounding in love and faithfulness" (Exodus 34:6).

God may care about others, but he doesn't care about me. Another way of putting this is, "I'm different. I'm special. I'm unlovable." This warped impression of being "special" is part of the false pride associated with an eating disorder. This false pride is used as a faulty rationale for staying with the behaviors of the eating disorder instead of submitting to God and crying out to him for help. The truth is you are special to God and he does care about you. Listen to this promise from Job 36:15-16: "But those who suffer he delivers in their suffering; he speaks to them in their affliction. He is wooing you from the jaws of distress to a spacious place free from restriction, to the comfort of your table laden with choice food."

I can hide my eating disorder from God and handle it on my own. Ever since Adam and Eve tried to hide from God in Eden, we have been thinking we can keep secrets from God. I cannot count the number of times I have heard this thought expressed by someone struggling with an eating disorder. There is nothing that is secret from God, and an eating disorder is not a thing to handle on your own. "'Can anyone hide in secret places so that I cannot see him?' declares the LORD. 'Do not I fill heaven and earth?' declares the LORD" (Jeremiah 23:24).

Your Earthly Father

If you have never established a satisfying relationship with your heavenly Father, your difficulty might stem from a negative, distorted relationship with your earthly father. If your earthly father was demanding and perfectionistic, you may imagine God as a wrathful, rigid dispenser of justice. If the only love your human father offered you was conditional, then you may see God's love as nearly unattainable. If your earthly father was emotionally distant, then you probably visualize God as an uncaring superbeing unconcerned with mere mortals.

None of these descriptions present an accurate portrait of God. You need to look beyond your own father, with all his mistakes and failures, and allow the perfect Father to paint his own portrait. "You see, at just the right time, when we were still powerless, Christ died for the ungodly.... But God demonstrates his own love for us in this: While we were still sinners, Christ died for us" (Romans 5:6,8).

THE TRUE FATHER

In all his dealings with us, God colors himself with love and grace. Accept that God loves you right where you are, eating disorder and all. If you grew up in a situation where you had to earn love, you may feel that you need to be perfect, cured, before God can love you. God fully recognizes our inability to attain perfection on our own, which is why he provided us with his own perfection through the life of his Son. If you want to seek perfection before God, seek it through Jesus Christ, who offers us the unconditional gift of grace.

You may harbor resentment toward God and feel that he is responsible for your eating disorder. You may have prayed to him countless times for help in overcoming it. You may even hate God for not taking your disorder away.

God is aware of your problem, but he is not the cause of it. He does not desire for it to continue, but that does not mean that you should expect him to "zap" it out of existence. God often calls his children to complete a journey instead of miraculously transporting them to their destination, because it is along the way that lessons are learned and insights are gained. He can, however, give you the help and strength you need to complete that journey, if you'll let him.

If you don't consider yourself to be a religious person, at least consider acknowledging that you have a spiritual side. Often people refer to God as a "Higher Power." However you view God, understand spiritual help is available that can be of great value on your journey.

Not only is God's strength available, but God's example of forgiveness is available. Confronted by the pain of your past, you may be finding it hard to forgive the people who hurt you. Look to God to show you the way. Through his forgiveness, described in the Bible, you can find the ability to forgive others. Christ died so that we might be forgiven by God. That forgiveness is given to us even though we don't deserve it. That's what God's grace is all about. If you can learn to accept God's grace and forgive yourself, you will also begin to be able to forgive those who have hurt you.

Many of you reading this have religious backgrounds of some sort. You may have learned enough of God from your upbringing to be scared to death of him. But remember: The people who showed you this wrathful, judgmental God could very well be the same people who are responsible for the pain behind your eating disorder. Your understanding of God may come from them. In many ways, their understanding was lacking.

Just as you must put the past in the proper perspective to understand it more fully, you also need to put God and your understanding of him in the proper perspective. God is larger, more merciful, infinitely more compassionate, and more willing to dispense grace than you can begin to imagine. I heartily recommend that you get a readable Bible in a contemporary translation, and look again at who God is. Allow him to reveal himself to you. It's time to break away from someone else's understanding of God and establish an understanding of your own.

Spiritual Well-Being

No matter what your spiritual past has been, you can actively define a new spiritual well-being. One of the most effective ways to integrate a new spiritual well-being is to verbalize new truths about God and about yourself. Say the following statements aloud whenever you feel your spiritual well-being undermined:

- I have value. (Say it even if you don't feel it or believe it at the time.)
- I am loved by God. (Say it even if you don't feel like it or haven't experienced it.)
- Because God loves me, I have hope. (Say it even if hope seems distant.)
- I can experience healing. (Say it even if you don't understand what healing will mean.)
- I can talk to God. (Say all these things to yourself, and then say them to God.)

That last point can be particularly scary for those who have not been in the habit of regular conversation with God. If this describes you, a wonderful place to start learning about an honest, forthright conversation with God is through the book of Psalms. There, David recorded heartfelt, open prayers to God. Like him, you can tell God how you feel. Talk to him. Question him. Cry out to him.

(If you do not have a Bible, or if you are looking for a companion Bible, consider *The Soul Care Bible,* edited by Dr. Tim Clinton, president of the American Christian Counselors Association. This wonderful resource is specially annotated for those in recovery from serious struggles, including eating disorders.)

FOOD FOR THOUGHT

My Image of God

1. When I was growing up, God was always presented as being…

    My parents may have presented themselves as being religious, but at home they acted differently in the following ways:

    Going to church as a child made me feel…

2. Here are the ways in which my view of God coincides with my own father's personality:

3. God says he forgives people, but I've never felt like I could expect forgiveness because I've…

    God has had no real place in my life because…

    I've always felt God couldn't love me because…

    It's hard for me to connect with God's forgiveness while I still…

    I'm angry with God because…

4. The times in my life when I've felt really close to God and felt like he heard me are:

    The times in my life when I've felt separated from God and felt like he didn't care are:

    I'm afraid to think that God would really care for me, because then it would mean that I…

5. Whatever your religious background, take some time to think about what you've always heard or been taught about God. Now think about what you've always wanted to be true about God. Often people who profess no religious faith at all will find

themselves praying in times of crisis, on the off-chance that maybe God does exist. Whether you believe in him or not, he is real, and he desires a relationship with you.

6. You've written letters to those who have hurt you. Now it's time to write a prayer. God desires honesty. Tell him anything you want— what you're thinking or even that you don't really believe he exists. (It won't be the first time he's heard that.) Tell him what you're feeling. Ask him for what you want. Plead with him for what you need. Expect him to live up to his promises.

7. If you are unfamiliar with prayer, or with speaking your heart directly to God, pick up the Bible and turn to Psalms. Read several of the psalms at random. Let your heart guide you as you turn the pages. Allow God to speak to you through the words of David. Use David's conversations with God through the psalms as an example of prayer.

If you feel able, write your prayer in the form of a psalm.

IN THE RIGHT DIRECTION

THE REAL MEANING OF FAITH

In the world today, faith and an acceptance of God are often derided as outdated and old-fashioned, crutches used by less capable people. If you have bought into this reasoning and think that God really has no part in your life, think about the kind of world that convinced you of this. It is also the world that told you that physical appearances were more important than the person you are inside. It is the world that permits abuse on all levels. It is also the world that measures success by the size of one's salary. In the light of this track record, I ask that you allow God himself to explain why you need him.

If you grew up hearing about a distant, perfectionistic, judgmental God, I urge you again to reexamine the Creator of the universe. Exchange your false view of God for the divine perspective.

Please go online to www.aplaceofhope.com/audio/poweroffaith.html for my special message on the power of faith.

For some, there is an acceptance of God but a rejection of Christ. But to reject Christ is to reject the personification of God's love and acceptance.

Please, pick up a Bible. Open its pages and let God speak to you. But be quiet and listen carefully for his voice. The world with all its noise will try to drown him out. Don't let it.

Affirming Action

There is great joy to be found in pursuing your own personal understanding of who God is. You have an opportunity to begin a spiritual quest into the very nature of the God of the universe, a God who knows you by name and loves you with a steadfast, enduring love. Don't let other people tell you who God is. Don't let other people distort who you think you are to God. Don't let fear paralyze you. Don't let anger distract you.

Instead, be guided by faith, hope, and love. Stand honestly as a person of faith and as a person with an eating disorder during this search; God does not expect you to be other than you are. He accepts you as you are, eating disorder included.

But it is his desire for you to take this journey. At the end of the journey, his desire is for the person of faith to remain.

Father, perfect Father, here I am. It is your child, [speak your name before God here]. I have so needed you to love me. Reveal your love to me each day. Give me hope for my future and healing for my pain. Strengthen me to know you better and to trust your love for me.

I want to know who you are. I need to know from you who I am.

Sixteen

Learning to Live

"Who do you want to be today?"

The question spoke the promise of the possible. It opened the door to vision and dreams. Three years ago, the question would have made no sense at all to Rachel. Then, what she wanted was of little relevance. Her actions, her life, had been dictated by her eating disorder. Then, today was just like yesterday and just like a joyless tomorrow.

"Who do you want to be tomorrow?"

Rachel smiled. "I don't know yet about tomorrow," she answered, "but I know who I want to be today. Today, I'm going to be me. And that's going to be good enough."

Somewhere along the line, Rachel decided to like herself again. She didn't have great plans for tomorrow yet. For now, it was enough to get up in the morning, look at herself in the mirror, and smile. For now, it was enough to forgive herself for the small stuff and be honest about the big stuff.

"Today, I'm going to be me," she decided, "and tomorrow I'm going to be more." That idea was also new—the idea of growth, not merely fighting to keep from being less. She'd traded in growth for the cocoon of her eating disorder. After three years, Rachel was ready to emerge.

Tomorrow I'm going to be more held such promise for Rachel. Tomorrow was something she could anticipate instead of dread. What would she learn? Who would she meet? Life, she was learning, was discovery, not drudgery.

"I'll tell you who I'm not today and won't be tomorrow," she ventured. "I'm not now, nor will I ever be, perfect." And then she smiled and hugged herself.

This must be how release from captivity feels, Rachel thought. She'd imprisoned herself within herself. Through hard work, perseverance, prayer, and the patience of the person sitting across from her, she'd found the keys to unlock the doors.

A thought came to Rachel just then. She looked up and asked, "Who do *you* want to be tomorrow?" And took another step beyond.

LIVING, NOT SURVIVING

You have probably lost touch with what it means to enjoy life. As you've struggled with your eating disorder, most of your time has been spent simply surviving. Now that you've begun your journey toward health and wholeness, you can start to think about living—and enjoying life—again.

Accepting your past and forgiving others for causing you pain is allowing you to accept and forgive yourself. When you accept yourself, you can laugh again—at yourself and others. Your happiness will no longer be based on the opinions and desires of other people. Fear of being rejected will no longer hold you prisoner, because you no longer reject yourself and your past. You are learning to really *like* who you are. You have learned that it's okay and perfectly normal to make mistakes.

Relearning Intimacy

Freed from the bondage of outside opinion, you'll be able to risk yourself by giving yourself to others. Because of your eating disorder, you've been isolated from those around you. This isolation has been largely due to fear—fear that others will discover what you do, fear that they will find out who you really are, and fear of your own unresolved anger. Understanding casts out fear. Anchored solidly in your understanding and self-acceptance, you can begin to trust other people again.

Now comes the time to reestablish the joys of intimacy. When you are comfortable with your own body, you can enjoy being with another person and allow him or her to enjoy your body as well. Once you've understood the nature of past abuses and how they've led you to lean on faulty behaviors, you will be free to relearn proper relationships and expressions of love, especially physical love.

You'll finally be able to come out from behind your mask and present an honest face to yourself and others. It's okay to show the world who you really are. Some people will still reject you, but others will accept you. Seek these people out. Find friends who will help you celebrate who you are now and who you are becoming.

As you go about strengthening, reestablishing, and developing relation-ships, it is important to remember the following guidelines.

Be honest with your feelings. This does not mean your relationships must be solely dictated by your feelings and emotions. But through your eating disorder, you have developed a pattern of covering over or numbing your emotions. One of the joys of a relationship is the ability to experience a full range of emotions within the context of another person. Expect to experience a variety of feelings. This is normal.

Develop clear boundaries. Relationships are not invitations for others to take advantage of you. Healthy relationships are mutually uplifting and edi-fying. Pick and choose your relationships carefully, and find people who will honor and respect your boundaries. Be sure, also, to honor and respect their boundaries.

Respond rather than react when you are hurt. Your eating disorder has been a reaction to pain in your life. Even though your eating disorder may be com-ing to an end, pain in life is not. Relationships involve hurt. Becoming in-volved with imperfect people means you will be hurt. Remember, however, that being imperfect yourself, you will also cause hurt. That is why forgive-ness must well up like an ongoing fountain in your life.

Forgiveness is a response to pain in your life, but it is by no means the only response you can choose. For responding really means choosing, and choosing allows *you* to be in control instead of your eating disorder. Work to develop and select healthy responses that are effective for you and do not hurt others. These responses may range from outright forgiveness to reevaluating the desirability of a relationship.

Seek maturity in your relationships. Sometimes when we have been hurt, we are so focused on our own pain that we use it to excuse our own hurtful behavior. It's as if we are saying, "It's beyond my ability to act differently because of what I've been through. Besides, your pain is nothing compared to my pain." Use your experiences for good and not evil. Use the pain you have suffered to strengthen your compassion and empathy for others. Let your pain add to your relationship instead of detracting from it.

All of us have been hurt and all of us cause pain; it's the nature of who we are as human beings. The point is not to avoid relationships in order to avoid pain. Instead, the goal is to learn from our pain and grow as individuals dedicated to reducing the amount and severity of the pain we cause others and ourselves. This is maturity. An eating disorder freezes you at the point of self-absorbed emotional adolescence, encouraging you to do whatever is necessary to feel better momentarily. Seek to respond in your relationships in a mature way.

Your eating disorder has been demoralizing you for too long, draining you of your self-respect, numbing all of your emotions. Now, freed from the bondage of the past, expect to feel laughter, sadness, surprise, honest anger, and cleansing tears. Learning to live means reexperiencing and dealing with all the rush of emotions given to you by your Creator. As if you were blind and suddenly given sight, you will be free to *feel* the world again.

This is a world where loving, laughing, and living are possible. Instead of being inwardly directed, intent on survival, you'll be outwardly directed, enjoying relationships with others.

You 101

Alfred Adler, called by many the father of individual psychotherapy, taught that all behavior has a goal. We base our actions on how those actions serve a purpose for us. In the past, you have chosen to engage in your eating disorder because you believed it would give you certain results. It is my fervent hope that, at this point, you can honestly say that your eating disorder is not delivering and is actually a severe detriment to your life and well-being. You can now decide to discontinue your eating disorder and seek other, beneficial ways to meet your needs. You can now decide to live free from your eating disorder and rediscover who you really are.

Learning to live again means relearning many of the basic skills and emotions you were unable to fully develop in childhood. Knowing how to be angry and how to properly express that anger are two of the most important things you will need to relearn. Honesty and openness, instead of secret-keeping and deception, must also be practiced.

Learning to live means living in the real world. Your fantasy world of childhood, with its "if onlys," must be jettisoned for the truth. Looking at yourself and those around you without the distortion of your eating disorder will free you from the delusions of the past.

You will also have to learn to deal with relapses. Stripped of the predictable behaviors of your eating disorder, you may feel naked when confronted with difficult situations. Expect this. Don't panic because of it. Your perfectionism will want to tell you that a momentary lapse spells failure forever. Don't listen! Perfect recovery should not be expected; consistent progress is your goal.

The Joy of Life

- Enjoyment of simple pleasures
- The return of laughter
- Allowing for the mistakes of yourself and others
- Developing intimacy
- Vision for who you are and what you can become

To help, think about what your "pressure points" are, those situations that are most likely to reignite your desire to return to old, faulty behaviors. Avoid those situations whenever possible. If avoidance isn't possible, substitute a healthy response instead of the response of your eating disorder. Choose to respond differently.

The life of every person is precious, and no one is ever too old to learn. No matter how long your behavior has been going on, you can come to a fuller understanding of who you are and why you do what you do—and effect positive changes in your life.

There's no way to physically go back and remake the past. But the hurt and lonely child you were then can be comforted by the adult you are today. Your misunderstood child can be recognized by you today. The love and comfort denied you in the past, even if never provided by those who hurt you, can still be given by your perfect Father, who stands ready to shower you with infinite love.

Surviving isn't enough. Existing isn't enough. Coping isn't enough. Life awaits you if you are willing to learn—about your past and what really happened, about your present and who you are now, and about your future and who you can become.

FOOD FOR THOUGHT

Learning to Live Again

Learning to live means, among other things, learning to:

- like yourself again.
- give yourself openly to others.
- experience emotions—especially anger—appropriately.
- live successfully in the real world with its day-to-day stresses.

1. What else does learning to live mean to me?

2. Things I like about who I am:

When I was _____, I liked who I was because...

I've learned I don't have to be perfect and can make mistakes because...

3. The following are my positive physical attributes:

   My definition of intimacy and what it encompasses is:

   In order to be intimate with another person, I need to...

4. As I become more familiar with my past and with the reasons behind my eating disorder, I find I am feeling more...

   Emotions I'm beginning to feel again include:

5. When I get angry, I still want to...

   When I get angry, my healthy way to express it will be to...

   When I'm angry now, I'll still need to watch out for the following reactions:

6. When I have a relapse, the first thing I'm going to do is...

   The second thing I'm going to do is...

7. My "pressure points" are:

   The people I need to stay away from right now are:

   If I absolutely cannot avoid some of my "pressure points," here are my strategies for how I'm going to deal with those situations or people:

8. Who I am today:

   Who I am becoming:

Living in an eating-disordered world has been an existence of shadows and gray. Your life should begin to take on new color and vibrancy now. Expect to start seeing your surroundings in a different light. Expect to feel new and dawning emotions.

9. It's time to get your "child," your doll, and go for a walk. If you're uncomfortable taking your doll with you, go without it, but remember, you're trying to get away from being so concerned over what other people think. In all probability, most people won't give your doll more than a passing thought. If they do, it might make for interesting conversation—if you're ready. Otherwise, just smile pleasantly and walk on.

10. Make sure to note the way things look, smell, feel, sound, and taste. Open up all your senses to really experience the world around you. Make sure to note also how you are feeling. Bring this book and your journal along, or have them handy when you return so you can jot down what you experienced—both outside of yourself and within.

11. Close your eyes and imagine that you are being interviewed on your hundredth birthday. What are the top five things you have accomplished?

IN THE RIGHT DIRECTION

STEPPING OUT IN FAITH

Consider these words from Anne Frank, a young teenager caught in the insanity of the Nazi Holocaust. In the midst of incomprehensible depravity and cruelty of one person to another, she remained a buoyant, hopeful soul.

She was able to see beyond the terror of today and into the promise of tomorrow. May her example give you strength.

> Every day I feel myself maturing, I feel liberation drawing near,
> I feel the beauty of nature and the goodness of the people around
> me…. With all that, why should I despair?[1]

There's a whole new world out there, waiting for you to discover it. It's a world where laughter and love are possible and where tears and grief are too. It's a world of both sunshine and rain. Both are needed if you are to grow.

You have the wonderful job of learning how to love yourself again. All this time, you've been searching for two elusive things—love and acceptance.

Before, you counted on others to provide them for you. In your new reality, you can provide those things for yourself. When you accept yourself, others will follow. People you meet will take their lead from you in how you want to be treated. If you present them with a person worthy of your own love and acceptance, they will be more willing to give you their love and acceptance in return.

Before, relationships must have seemed to you like jumping off a cliff. In your new reality, they may still feel that way. But this time, you'll be firmly anchored to your own sense of self. If you fall, you'll have the rope of your own self-acceptance to climb back up on.

Your new reality will not be without risk or relapse. As with any new skill, there will be the inevitable backward step. This need not be a signal for full retreat. Pick yourself up and go forward again. After you've done that, take a look back at where you've been and really ask yourself if that's where you want to end up. Then turn yourself back around and continue forward.

AFFIRMING ACTION

> "For I know the plans I have for you," declares the LORD,
> "plans to prosper you and not to harm you, plans to give you

hope and a future. Then you will call upon me and come and pray to me, and I will listen to you. You will seek me and find me when you seek me with all your heart. I will be found by you," declares the LORD, "and will bring you back from captivity." (Jeremiah 29:11-14)

Believe God's promise. Believe in his ability to bring you back from the captivity of your eating disorder. Believe in your future. Believe in his love. Trust it and hold on to it tightly.

God, I am not here by accident or mistake. You have plans for me and a future of hope and promise. God, I am moving toward my positive future. Be with me each step of the way. Help me learn to live again, to love again, to laugh again.

Seventeen

Letting Others Inside

"Hi, Lauren, it's Jennie. I was wondering if you wanted to go to a movie or something with me." Lauren faced a dilemma: how to answer. Part of her wanted to make up a good excuse and say no. She was having a bad day and wanted to stay home, locked away in her misery. But Jennie deserved more. Lauren had told Jennie the truth and, in doing so, had given Jennie the right to expect the truth from her.

So, in truth, Lauren answered, "I don't know. I'm not doing so good today." She still felt guilty telling Jennie the truth. She knew that when she did, she transferred some of her burden over to Jennie. More than anything, she had always avoided being a burden to others. It had been so hard to accept that Jennie was willing, out of love, to shoulder some of her burden.

Lauren was learning about the depth of friendship. It was frightening to her at first. Friendship meant diffusing the anger she held so tightly inside. It meant giving in to hope and accepting the possibility of healing. It meant giving up the isolation of her eating disorder. At first, in an odd way, friendship had been about loss.

In order to have a friendship with Jennie, Lauren had to surrender her singular relationship with her eating disorder. Jennie expected Lauren to turn to her—not to her eating disorder—for comfort. Jennie expected Lauren to heal. Lauren had run from the expectations of others; it felt risky to put herself in that position again. It also felt good.

On the other end of the line, Jennie smiled. She was relieved. Lauren didn't try to hide what was really going on. Before Jennie called, she had prayed for Lauren to have the strength to open up to her. When Lauren didn't tell her the truth, she rejected their friendship. Jennie understood the rejection and didn't let it deter her. Patiently, lovingly, she made herself available to Lauren.

For Jennie lived with the hope that Lauren would move into a full, reciprocal friendship, the way it used to be when they were younger. She was willing to accept that for now Lauren's eating disorder would dominate the friendship. How could it not? It had been slowly destroying her friend. For too long she'd been reluctant to say anything, to share with Lauren her suspicions and her fears. She had so wanted them not to be true. Finally, she could stay silent no longer. She had to decide if she loved the silence more than she loved Lauren. She chose Lauren.

So they talked. And Lauren explained to Jennie why she was having a bad day and how she was feeling. Jennie tried very hard to understand when she could. And when she didn't understand, she just listened. Against the battering of Lauren's self-doubt and anger, Jennie relentlessly presented the bulwark of her own acceptance and love. As Lauren talked, Jennie could see why she was having a rough day. Mentally squaring her shoulders, she prepared to take on a greater load.

"So," Lauren said after a long pause, "how's your day going today?" And the load got lighter.

ALLOWING OTHERS TO HELP YOU

An important part of your recovery involves reaching out to others for love and support. The shame, distress, and lack of self-control and self-worth you felt because of your eating disorder have gradually isolated you from your friends and family members. Now it is time to break out of that circle of loneliness and get the help you need. Our heavenly Father put us on this earth to help one another, and you need to trust that others will open up to you even as you open up your heart to them.

It is important, however, that you make it clear to others that you are not expecting them to fix you, criticize you, or judge you according to their value system. Instead, you are asking them for love, acceptance, and understanding. If they are to truly help you, it will be necessary for them to educate themselves about your eating disorder. It will also be necessary for you to clearly articulate your needs and feelings every step of the way.

Consider the following guidelines as you reach out to others for help.

1. *Be clear and fair.* Others, even those nearest to you, will not always be able to help you exactly as you would like. Resist the tendency to try to control how they help you. Give grace.

2. *Model respect by being respectful to those near you.* Use the language of respect in your dealings with others. Don't allow fear, anger, shame, or guilt to keep you from saying, "Thank you," "I appreciate all you've done," "I love you." Remove insults and sarcastic comments from your speech. Avoid using your friends and loved ones for target practice with verbal arrows.

3. *Have appropriate limits for how much you allow others to do for you.* Real love includes having appropriate limits. An eating disorder can be a strong vacuum, sucking others into a caretaking role. You must learn to care for yourself, without your eating disorder, and this caretaking can produce resentments in the long run. The goal in friendship is interdependence, not dependence.

4. *Use the fruit of the Spirit as your relational guide.* "But the fruit of the Spirit is love, joy, peace, patience, kindness, goodness, faithfulness, gentleness and self-control" (Galatians 5:22-23). Seek to give and to receive these attributes in your relationships. Use them as a guide to determine the health of your relationships.

5. *Actively redefine who you are.* As you are actively changing your behaviors, you can drop words like *dysfunctional* and *codependent.* Defining yourself by these terms can be an excuse not to change. Try using words like *recovering* and *growing.*

6. *Accept responsibility for your eating disorder.* No matter what kind of childhood past you have had, remember that parents and others are not the only cause of your eating disorder. You yourself bear responsibility for the choices you have made and are making. Take responsibility for yourself and for your relationships. As you take responsibility, you will be able to eliminate the blame.

REACHING OUT

To help you to reach out, ask for help, and truly communicate what you need for your recovery, I have included nine positive steps others can take to assist you. I have placed these nine steps in a letter and suggest that you share this letter with friends or family members you want to ask for help. Then discuss it with them.

Following this letter is a section written especially for those who want to help you in your recovery. You may wish to read and discuss this section together as well.

Dear _____,

I am asking for your love, support, and understanding as I recover from my eating disorder. To enable you to help me better, I have listed nine positive steps that I would like you to keep in mind. I think it would be especially valuable for you and me to discuss these ideas after you have finished reading them.

1. Please understand that you cannot "fix" me. It is important for you to resist this tendency at all costs. This healing journey must be mine alone to take. You can help me on my way, but you cannot walk it for me.

2. Please operate from a position of acceptance. This does not mean that you agree with my behavior; it means that you accept my behavior as my way of coping with some sort of pain.

Condemning me for choosing this faulty mechanism will only add to my pain and loss of self-esteem.

3. Please read all you can on the subject. Be familiar with the treatment programs and therapy methods available.

4. Please allow me to talk about my disorder without placing the burden of judgment onto my shoulders. Operate from a position of love and concern for me. Make it "safe" for me to talk to you.

5. After we have talked, avoid minimizing my pain and experiences. My problem may seem so clear to you that you may be tempted to offer pat answers and instant solutions. Just remember, I have experienced years of suffering and aloneness. Pat answers may only reinforce my suspicion that no one understands. It would help me most if you could just listen to my feelings and emotions without making value judgments.

6. If you are one of the people I hold responsible for the pain in my life, please try not to react with hostility and defensiveness when I share my memories of the past with you. Accept my version of events and how I feel about what happened, even if you remember things differently. Allow me to work through my healing journey and come to the point where I understand my need to forgive you. Don't try to force me to understand your point of view at this stage. I'll eventually reach the point where I can listen to you.

7. Guard against becoming my "warden," policing my actions, and making demands on me. Fear of the damage I am doing to myself may entice you to want to get a handle on my behavior quickly. But trying to force me may increase the destructive behaviors. I need to be loved, not forced, in order to change.

Also, be careful not to monitor what I eat, discuss my food intake with me, or ask me how much I weigh. You cannot will me to get better by using your own will to supersede mine. I *want* to get better, but I must be allowed to make decisions on my own.

8. *Don't feel as if you have to back down in a conflict.* State your opinion, clearly and honestly, but state it as an *opinion.* Allow for differences of opinion between us.

9. *Finally, please understand that my behavior took time to develop, and I must also be allowed time to accomplish my healing journey.* Pressuring me to "get well soon" will only retard my progress.

Thank you for caring enough to listen and help. I need your understanding and support very much as I continue on my journey to recovery.

Sincerely, _____

How to Help

At the core of all these steps is *loving* the individual. (To avoid awkwardness, I will assume that the individual is female, though of course this is not always the case.) Loving the individual means doing what is best for her, not what will make you feel better. She needs to be allowed to express her anger and her pain, even if it is painful for you.

While dealing with an eating-disordered friend or loved one, it is important not to neglect the other relationships in your life. If the person is someone in your family, focusing solely on her may strain your relationship with your spouse or others in the family, especially other children. Dwelling exclusively on the eating-disordered individual can damage the rest of the family. It is a "family" problem, but it need not destroy the family.

Also be aware that your actions and attitudes are very important to the one with the eating disorder. If she is a member of your family, what you think about her is essential to her. If she is a friend, she needs your love and acceptance. It is especially important not to compare her with other people, especially siblings. Her self-esteem is already in question; it doesn't need to be battered further by unfair comparisons.

Constant questions of "How are you doing?" "How are you feeling?" or "How is it going?" can aggravate the eating-disordered person's feeling of inadequacy. She may have numbed her feelings for so long that she is unable to articulate exactly what she is feeling. Allow her to tell you what she wants, when she wants. Being open and honest are new skills that she is mastering. Let her work into them as she continues on her journey.

Along with loving the individual comes trusting the individual. She must be allowed to find her own values, her own ideals and standards, and her own answers, rather than being required to accept yours.

Be willing to go into therapy with her if she feels you are responsible for her pain. Working together to come to a knowledge and acceptance of the truth can establish a pattern of relationship that will last long after the therapy is over.

Whether family or friend, someone with an eating disorder desperately needs people around her who love and accept her. She needs the safety of that love and acceptance to venture out into the reality of her painful past. Being there for her, accepting her, and listening to her can give her the support she needs.

Teaming Together

As you work together to establish, strengthen, and maintain relationships, keep the following in mind.

- Allow each other to have your own opinions and feelings.
- Accept that the other person brings a sincere heart to the friendship.
- Practice sharing about other things in life besides food, weight, and eating disorder–related topics.
- Practice intentional listening by putting aside your own assumptions about what the other person is saying and listening for what they mean.
- Give and receive positive feedback.
- Ask for prayer and pray for each other.
- Articulate your hope for the future.
- Begin to incorporate food as a part of your friendship, without making food the center of attention.

- Verbalize forgiveness by saying, "I forgive you" and "I'm sorry."
- Resolve your anger and avoid hostile "loose ends."
- Refuse to accept or impose unrealistic guilt.
- Participate in social and relational bonding activities together.
- Practice love with limits by respecting appropriate boundaries with each other.

Reestablishing relationships is vital to recovery from an eating disorder. Dealing with other people, however, can be messy. They have different opinions. They mess up and don't always act the way you need them to act. Relationships can appear risky when compared to the predictable results from your eating disorder. You must resist the temptation to view your eating disorder as a superior relationship. It is not. People are worth the effort. Love is worth the trouble. Reconciliation is worth the forgiveness.

FOOD FOR THOUGHT

Asking for Help in Recovery

Take another look at the example letter in this chapter. What is included is by no means a complete list of all the things you might wish to say. In my experience, however, those I have listed have proved to be vital in establishing a healing relationship. Please take some time to put into perspective why each step is so positive in your own recovery.

1. Why step 1 is important to me:

2. Step 2 would be necessary for those who love me because…

3. Reasons for step 3:

4. If _____ could do step 4, it would mean…

5. Step 5 is especially important to me because…

6. I need _____ to understand step 6 because...

7. What step 7 means to me:

8. Step 8 makes me feel...

9. I need step 9 for the following reasons:

10. Additional steps that would help me:

11. Now may be the time for you to allow another loving friend or family member to join you on your journey. First, have them read as many of the chapters in this book as you feel necessary. Then, together, review as much of the "Food for Thought" sections as you feel comfortable sharing.

    If you're not ready yet to include others in your recovery (besides the friend or professional who has been with you all along), that may be a future goal for you. First, write down who you want to have work with you. Second, write down who you need to have work with you. Remember, the person you are thinking of may accept this idea or reject it. You're not responsible for his or her response. Also, write down why you are ready to include some people but not necessarily others.

    I want the following person(s) to work with me because...

    The following person(s) need(s) to hear what I have to say because...

    I'm ready to share my journey with those I've listed because...

    Sharing with the others I've listed doesn't feel comfortable to me right now because...

    If the following things were to happen, then I might feel comfortable sharing my writings and drawings with them:

IN THE RIGHT DIRECTION

COMING OUT OF EXILE

It is said that no one is an island, yet through your disorder you've separated yourself from other people. To control your surroundings, you couldn't afford to include other people in your life—because people are notoriously unpredictable and often uncontrollable. Over time you've walled yourself in. Now it's time to start dismantling your wall, brick by brick.

One of the first bricks you need to remove is the one that hides your disorder from those who truly love you. They need to see what this has been doing to you. You need to allow them the opportunity to help you.

If you are a perfectionist, that attitude has fostered a solitary state of mind within you. Perfectionism demands private effort and rewards

A Special Message from Dr. Gregg Jantz

Believe in your recovery.

Believe in today.

Believe that God loves you.

Believe that your life makes a difference.

Believe there is light at the end of the tunnel.

Believe you are the light for someone else who needs hope.

Believe that the best is yet to be.

Believe in yourself.

I believe in you...

accomplishments privately. Part of you may not want to include others in your recovery to avoid being indebted to them in any way: *It's my disorder, so it should be my cure.* This attitude only strengthens your perfectionism and false pride—and neither one will assist your recovery.

This chapter urged caring family and friends to give you two things you desperately need: love and trust. Those who are deeply concerned about you may want to give you that love and trust as desperately as you need to receive it. Take the chance. Open up to someone, but be wise about the choice. Choose someone who loves you, and then allow that person to show you how much. Both of you will benefit.

AFFIRMING ACTION

The time to remain trapped with your disorder is over. Freedom awaits you. And included in that freedom is the reality of unpredictability. You have already decided that you do not want to continue living in the past. You have already decided that you want the future to look different than it does today. You have already acknowledged that hope is more important than control. Please, don't forget what you've learned.

Life is worth the chance. Love is worth the risk. God is sufficient.

Dear God, open my heart to love and be loved. Send me people who will love me as you do. Help me to grow in my love for others. Help me to love other people more than I do food. Help me to love freedom more than slavery. Help me to trust you to take care of my future.

General Questions on Eating Disorders

What is the difference between compulsive overeating and an eating disorder?

An eating disorder is a food addiction, with emotional roots and a physiological component that leads to cravings, leading to an unbalancing of your body chemistry. If you overeat, that does not necessarily mean you have an eating disorder. Everyone overeats occasionally. If you overeat compulsively, this can turn into disordered eating, which can develop into an eating disorder. An eating disorder happens when you go to extremes with food, or if you go to food to escape unpleasant situations or to deal with emotions of anger, fear, or guilt. This is where you cross the line from compulsive eating to disordered eating to an eating disorder.

Are eating disorders inherited?

There has been some fairly recent, although inconclusive, research that looked at this question of whether or not eating disorders are genetic or biological in nature. In my experience, eating disorders are not inherited; rather, the faulty behaviors relating to food, body image, and dieting are inherited. You may have a predisposition towards an eating disorder because of the environment you've grown up in or because of abuse. It is a learned response, a coping mechanism that may come from your family situation but is not inherited. An unhealthy situation, usually within the family, is behind an eating disorder. Look for family dynamics, not DNA.

You've mentioned that most people struggling with an eating disorder have abuse in their past. I can't remember ever being physically or sexually abused. Is it possible to have an eating disorder without abuse being present?

There are reasons for every behavior. An eating disorder develops as a coping mechanism. The key is to determine why you feel it's necessary to cope and what it is you are trying to cope with. I believe that some sort of abuse or pain lies at the heart of every eating disorder. It may have been blatant, such as sexual abuse; or it may have been subtle, such as verbal assaults on your self-esteem or self-worth; or it may have been unintentional, due to traumatic circumstances or unmet emotional needs. Emotional abuse may be hidden under years of denial, but it's there.

That said, I don't encourage people to spend the majority of their energy trying to unearth all of the specific events—to dig and dig and dig, getting stuck on the "why." The focus should be on understanding that the eating disorder is a result of unmet emotional needs or trauma and that food became a coping mechanism. This is a sufficient platform of understanding to begin the healing process.

I've used diet pills and/or laxatives for years and can't seem to get by without them. I vow every day not to take them, but I'll find myself going to the store to get them anyway. I'll even go to different stores so I won't be noticed. How do I get out from under my need for these pills?

Diet pills and laxatives are not only emotionally addictive; they are also extremely physically addictive—especially laxatives, which our intestinal tract and digestive system become dependent upon in order to operate. I suggest you work with a professional who understands addiction to diet pills and/or laxatives.

Sometimes it takes five or six months to help a person be weaned from laxative use. Laxatives need to be eliminated gradually, and it is very important to work with a professional to assist you in the proper timetable. In addition, a potassium chelate supplement may help. I've found that it usually takes thirty to sixty days to rid your system of diet pills and their residue. Getting over the mental addiction, however, may require an even longer amount of time.

I've had great difficulty finding a therapist who understands the role of nutrition in my eating disorder. Any suggestions for finding a professional who understands?

Many counselors claim to work with eating disorders, but very few use the whole-person approach to healing, which addresses the issues involved with the physical, emotional, relational, and spiritual health of the individual. Finding one person who is able to incorporate the whole-person model can be difficult. When making inquiries, it is important to ask people whether or not they have experience with eating disorders, what their philosophy of healing is, and whether or not they ascribe to a whole-person approach. See if they stress working with a team, as opposed to working alone.

Another important question to ask is how they view the use of supplements in the treatment of eating disorders. The research is becoming quite clear regarding the specific types of nutritional deficiencies experienced by those with eating disorders. Many of those with eating disorders have clinical levels of nutritional deficiencies; treating those deficiencies with specific supplements and formulas is the current standard of care.

Try to locate a prevention-minded physician who understands the role of nutrition in your disorder, and be totally honest. An environmental physician is also a good way to go, and such a professional will usually have knowledge of and training in nutrition. Have this physician work in conjunction with your therapist or counselor.

At The Center, our eating disorder clients who work with our nutritionist and medical personnel undergo an eating-disorder nutritional appraisal.

The information provided through this appraisal is used in treatment recommendations and continued care. (For more information about our eating-disorder nutrition appraisal, please contact us. We are able to assist you in completing this appraisal without the need for you to come to The Center in person.)

I suffer greatly from PMS. My physician has me on medication, but I notice I get intense urges to binge three to four days before my period. I tend to be a binge eater anyway, but it really intensifies during this time. Is there anything that can be done to help?

Cravings can be very intense before the onset of your period. There are physiological reasons for these cravings. Especially if you are a binge eater, one of the best things you can do to moderate these cravings is to go on a sound nutritional program to establish a pattern of giving your body the nutrients it needs in order to reduce the severity of the cravings. There are special formulas for PMS, one of which is called *Estroplex*. Another, mentioned earlier in this book, is a progesterone cream called *Profeminell*. Most PMS is due to high estrogen levels in the body, and the progesterone cream will have a significant effect on those who use it. It is a very safe formula, available over the counter.

In addition, many of our clients have been able to mitigate their PMS symptoms by supplementing their diet with B vitamins, as well as with a formula such as *Canditrol*. In addition to PMS you may also be suffering from a candida yeast infection. The demands of the yeast can produce intense cravings also.

A nutritionally oriented physician or nutritionist can help you find the physical reasons behind these cravings, allowing you the support you need to monitor the urge to binge.

I'm a Christian, and I feel God doesn't understand my eating disorder and hasn't saved me from it. I've begged and pleaded, prayed and prayed that the Lord would deliver me from this eating disorder; but I still find myself doing it. Can God help me? I feel like I've failed God!

Yes, God is able to help! God is helping right now! Delivery from an eating disorder is a process. It is not done overnight. But God is there with you through the healing journey.

One of the most important things for you to learn on this journey is to turn to God instead of to food. The pain is great, yet, through the intensity of the pain, God as the true answer becomes more clear. When the pain is beyond you, you must learn to seek beyond yourself for strength. The joy comes when you realize that, though the pain is beyond you, God is with you, ready to relieve you from your pain.

You must trust God to be with you, be patient with your progress, and be confident of your recovery. Specifically ask God to bless your efforts. Don't hold back a relationship with him until you're "healed." Place yourself firmly in his hands right now, right in the midst of your disorder. Be honest with him about what you are doing, how you are feeling, and what you need from him. Ask specifically for physical healing, so your body may heal. Ask that you would be inspired by him to care for your body. Request from him new passions for your life, a new purpose beyond your eating disorder.

Each day, ask for his help and express your gratitude for all he has done. Be expectant and hopeful. Ask God to help you live bravely each day. Ask him to bless all aspects of your recovery, from your past pain to your present body chemistry. Take some time and examine who God is to you and the role you believe he plays in your life. What are your expectations of God? Getting rid of the limited expectations you have toward him may allow him to work more fully in your life.

Often I'm asked if I think an eating disorder is a sin. I firmly believe that the sin is not the eating disorder. Doing nothing and choosing to remain in bondage to your eating disorder is the sin. Choosing slavery to the eating disorder over freedom in Christ is the sin. Choosing to worship food as an idol

over God is the sin. Remember, it's progress not perfection. When we are taking steps and efforts to heal, we will have progress. You can count on God!

Is it possible to control eating habits and still eat fast food?

Fast food usually means foods high in refined sugars, fats, and carbohydrates.
Usually it's difficult to control your eating habits and still eat these types of
food. However, the more you try to control these foods, the more you can
become obsessed with them. Does this mean that you have to give up French
fries for the rest of your life? No. But during recovery, it's best to focus on nutrition rather than diet. The more you eat a nutritionally balanced diet, use the
eating disorder supplements, and drink the appropriate amount of water each
day, the more your cravings for these foods will diminish. The more you experience emotional healing, the more these cravings will diminish also. Please try
to avoid such black-and-white thinking as never eating a certain type of food
again. Instead, focus on doing the good things nutritionally and what you are
gaining versus having a list of good and bad foods that you can or cannot eat.

When you do go out to eat at a fast-food restaurant, make healthier
choices. Many fast-food outlets include healthier selections on their menus.

The good news is that there is life after French fries! Even if you need to
give them up for a time, there are many other wonderful, healthy alternatives
to take their place. Accentuate the positive choices you are making in your
life and avoid concentrating on the negatives.

Do you believe Christians have more difficulty with eating disorders than non-Christians?

I believe that among Christian women eating disorders are often very secret
and hidden. Eating disorders can also seem more "acceptable" than alcohol,
drugs, or sexual addictions. The false guilt of restrictive religious beliefs may
inhibit seeking help. Some churches or religious settings are not conducive to
providing the help people need to recover from eating disorders.

Whenever I go to churches to speak about eating disorders, I try to encourage them to allow people within their congregation to bring their struggles into the light, to provide an atmosphere where people can be open with one another and find encouragement instead of condemnation. Eating disorders are strengthened by secrecy. Churches must foster an atmosphere of honesty, openness, and prayer for all those struggling.

It has also been my experience that food plays a major role in many church functions—from weddings and other events of great joy to funerals and events of great sadness. This reinforces the idea that food is a way of coping with the highs and lows of life.

It is my belief that while a rigid, faulty religious background can be a disadvantage to be overcome, religious beliefs can form a foundation for true, saving faith. The seeds of the true God can produce the fruits of strength, faith, and power for the one suffering from an eating disorder.

I've been using an antidepressant medication for my eating disorder. Are there any other options for me?

In my experience, antidepressants have not been overly effective for those with anorexia. However, if you are bulimic, some research has shown that antidepressant medication provides the most impressive short-term response rate of any treatment available. Medication may be needed for a while to help with depression. As the body is returned to a healthy balance, including important brain chemical functioning, the need for medication can significantly decrease. And while medication may be effective at alleviating symptoms, it cannot treat the underlying causes of an eating disorder. It cannot improve your self-esteem, resolve past and present conflicts, or teach you healthy coping skills.

If you're using an antidepressant, you should not go off it without consulting a physician first. You may, however, want to begin exploring adjunctive ways of dealing with your depression, such as nutritional supplementation. By doing so, you may find that you are able to experience a more comprehensive recovery.

How long does it take to get over an eating disorder?

In many cases, the answer depends upon how long you have suffered from the eating disorder. The longer the behavior, the longer it may take to recover. There are three things to look at:

- The type of help you are getting for your eating disorder. Are you taking a whole-person approach to your care? Are you incorporating the physical and spiritual components in your level of care?
- The type of support system you have to assist you in your recovery. It is especially important to develop healthy, wholesome relationships with others who will assist your recovery.
- The type of follow-up to support long-term recovery. Do you have a system of accountability and a long-term success strategy? What are you doing in the long run to assist in your recovery? Is there a strategy for the ongoing renewal of your mind and spirit?

At The Center, the first step to overcoming an eating disorder is our Intensive Outpatient Program. This typically consists of three to four weeks of daily, individualized treatment. During this short period of time, the work output can be similar to what can be accomplished in six months of weekly therapy. The "aftercare" program, created for each intensive client, is generally eighteen to twenty-four months. For some of the more severe forms of eating disorders, the range of care can be in the four- to five-year range, depending upon the level of abuse. This aftercare program generally begins with fairly frequent contact with The Center, which is reduced gradually as healing is realized. (For more information about our Intensive Outpatient Program, please contact us.)

FOOD FOR THOUGHT

Further Explorations

First, if you're having trouble identifying the type of abuse you suffered in the past, try making a timeline of your life. In your notebook or journal, map out the points in your life during which you felt hurt, rejected, abandoned, or lonely. Use anything you wish as a reference point: age, your grade in school, or other significant events.

This timeline can help you not only to identify the existence of abuse but also to determine what kind of abuse you suffered: physical, sexual, verbal, emotional, or a combination of all of these. If you cannot remember any abuse, do not try to make anything up. I am not encouraging you to construct memories, but rather to identify "hurt points." We've all had hurts of some type.

Second, if you have not already done so, you may want to consider finding a caring professional who can help you. If you already have a therapist or counselor, you may want to reevaluate your relationship to see if he or she is helping you in all the ways you need.

Take some time to write down what you want and need from your therapist/counselor/physician. Share these thoughts with your present counselor or with one you might consider working with in the future. What I need from my _____:

Third, if you are a Christian, you may have felt anger toward God for not responding to your cries for help. Read the following story and see how it might relate to you:

> A man was caught in a flood that threatened to wash his home
> away. As the water began to rise, he prayed fervently to God to
> deliver him from the rushing current. As soon as he stopped pray-
> ing, he noticed that the water had risen to the top of his front
> porch steps. A neighbor came by, rowing a small dinghy, and
> offered the man a ride out of danger.
>
> "No, thank you," the man replied. "I have prayed to God,
> and he will deliver me."
>
> When the water had climbed to the second story of his house,
> the man leaned out an upper window and saw a rescue worker

coming toward him in a motorboat. The worker urged the man to get into the boat and be saved from the flood.

"No, thank you," the man replied. "I have prayed to God, and he will deliver me."

Finally the rushing current had risen so high that the man had to climb onto the roof of his house or be swept away. As he sat there, a helicopter flew overhead, and a loud voice pleaded with the man to use the harness being lowered in order to escape from the torrent.

"No, thank you!" the man yelled over the roar of the water and propeller blades. "I have prayed to God, and he will deliver me!"

Not long after, the swell of the river engulfed the house completely, and the man drowned.

When he got to heaven, he was furious with God for not saving him.

"Why didn't you answer my prayers?" the man demanded angrily. "You could have saved me! Why didn't you?"

"I tried," the Lord responded. "I sent a rowboat, and you wouldn't get in. So I sent a motorboat, and still you wouldn't leave. Finally I sent a helicopter! You wouldn't get into any of them!"

If you have been focused on one way for God to save you, you may have missed opportunities sent your way. In order to assist you in expanding your vision, please do the following: Draw a dinghy, a motorboat, and a helicopter, or find pictures from your magazines. Label each as a person or event in your life that may have been sent by God to convince you to turn from your eating disorder and toward health.

Fourth, God does answer prayers—not always in just the way we envision the answer, but according to his will. Say the following prayer aloud, sending your petition to him:

Dear God,

I thank you that you love me. I thank you that you are intimately acquainted with every aspect of my life. You love me unconditionally and want to help me heal. As I continue this journey of self-awareness, please give me insight and understanding. Bring to my mind those things about my eating disorder that I need to know. Give me the courage to deal with them. Be with me in a special way as I desire healing and recovery from this eating disorder in my life. Restore my gratitude for all you have done, peace for all you are doing, and hope for all you will do.

Signed, _____

Date _____

IN THE RIGHT DIRECTION

GETTING THE HELP YOU NEED

No one book will be able to answer all the questions you have about your disorder. The more competent sources of information you can get, the better. That is why I feel it is vital for you to find or continue to work with a caring professional, if at all possible.

A caring professional not only can answer your questions but also can help you figure out which questions you need to ask. You can do a lot on your own toward your own recovery. In fact, the bulk of the work has to be yours. Working with the proper person, however, can point you in the direction you need to go, thus avoiding frustrating dead ends or energy-wasting circles.

Before you establish a relationship with anyone, ask some questions. Take this book with you. Use it as a yardstick to measure the capability of that individual to treat you as a whole person.

No one book will be able to answer all the questions you have about yourself. The most this one can do is to point out avenues of exploration. If you find that you've run into a dead end or are going around in circles, go back to a place where you were sure of your direction and start again. Expect to do this more than once. Everyone needs to stop and get their bearings now and again. By learning how to do this now, you'll be gaining yet another valuable life skill.

Questions About Anorexia and Bulimia

Do I have to get fat to get well?
Absolutely not. I cannot say this strongly enough. Obesity is just a different extreme of the eating disorder. We work to bring people to an efficient, appropriate weight, and what is healthy is different for each one. We work to reject the cookie-cutter image of the perfect weight projected through our body-conscious culture. Some will gain weight, and some will lose weight. For the anorexic, weight gain, if any, is gradual and usually one of the last aspects of therapy, because the fear is so great. Please don't worry; you will not become fat.

I've been out of control with an eating disorder for over seven years. I know I'm bulimic. I've felt such despair. I want to know: Can I ever really be happy?
Yes. I know because I've seen it happen for countless others. I've worked with people who have been bulimic for over thirty years, and I have watched them walk in freedom.

Personal happiness can be achieved at any point. We can say, "I am going to live in recovery. The eating disorder is no longer going to rob me of my personal happiness." This is a decision that helps you make the commitment to live differently, despite how you feel. This commitment involves doing everything it takes in order to live a life of wholeness, even though you may not always understand immediately what that means.

This decision requires great faith, and it requires assistance from other people, including—whenever possible—an eating disorder specialist. There are some wonderful organizations available to support a walk of recovery from an eating disorder. The International Association of Eating Disorder Professionals is an excellent resource and referral agency. In addition, the National Association of Anorexia Nervosa and Associated Disorders provides information and referrals for those with eating disorders. (See Appendix D for Web sites.)

I'm a recovering anorexic. I have lots of trouble with constipation and bloating. Every time I eat, I bloat up and feel horrible, so I would rather not eat! Is there anything I can do to become more comfortable with the food in my system?
Yes! Some of the greatest recent advances in the treatment of eating disorders is in the area of integrating nutrition into recovery. (The other is an increased recognition of the power of God's grace in healing from an eating disorder.)

As you are working toward healing, there will be times of discomfort. That is normal. But each day you give your body what it needs, you will experience relief from these more severe symptoms. It takes time and patience to allow your body to readjust to healthy functioning.

In order to rebalance your digestive system and move food through without negative symptoms, we use commercial supplements such as *Phase IV* and *Ultra Meal*, which are described earlier in this book. Taken together, these formulas allow your body to return to normal functioning, reducing periods of constipation and intestinal bloating.

It's important for you to have a nutritionist or a nutritionally oriented physician working with you during recovery. If you are suffering from this degree of constipation or bloating and you are not under the care of a trained professional, please contact us at The Center.

I have been bulimic for years and have started counseling. Is it possible I was a victim of sexual abuse and am just now recalling it?

Yes, it is possible. Over the years I've found that those things that you need to know in order to have healing and recovery will come naturally. You don't need to force, you don't have to make up, and you don't have to have any ideas implanted. But those things that happened to you, that you need to know, God will allow you to recall through the course of your recovery. And there will be healing. And there will be recovery.

Please, don't think you must focus on unearthing abuse. You don't need to search for hidden abuse, and you don't need to search always for "why, why, why?" The answers to these questions are not your destination, yet the search for them can become obsessive. What you can understand is that many times there have been traumatic events—or events that happened in your childhood that produced traumatic results due to your perspective—that are at the root of your eating disorder. It is not necessary to catalog each one in order to heal. Recovery is about moving beyond the behavior, whether or not you are able to dissect each reason for the behavior.

One of the greatest steps to recovery is recognizing that you developed an eating disorder as a way to cope with pain in your life. Starting today, you must decide to forgive the past and move on because you desire your life to be whole again.

I always seem to binge on a lot of sugar. I've suffered from bladder and yeast infections for years, along with my bulimia. Are my bladder and yeast infections due to my bulimia?

We have found the presence of candida, a yeast infection, in about 80 percent of our clients. Along with the presence of this yeast infection, they have a long history of bladder infections, as well as the range of PMS symptoms.

The good news is that candida is treatable. Many of our clients have attempted to control these recurring yeast and bladder infections through the use of antibiotics, with little or marginal success. We have found that a formula called *Canditrol* yields superior results for those with yeast infections due to an eating disorder.

I have been suffering in silence from an eating disorder. I know my mother has a long history of dieting, and I think she has an eating disorder too. We've never talked about our unusual relationship with food. Am I going to end up like my mom—obsessed with body image and always on a diet?

If you've watched your mother be restrictive in her eating and always on a diet, her behavior is a major factor in your own eating disorder. This does not mean, however, that the focus and the blame need to be on your mother. You can grow beyond these faulty attitudes.

According to the book *Like Mother, Like Daughter* by Debra Waterhouse, research shows that mothers who view their daughters as extensions of themselves are more controlling in areas where they themselves feel a lack of control. Hence, mothers who feel compelled to constantly control their own weight project that need for control onto their daughter's weight.

This hypercriticism by mothers of their daughters' weight and bodies does not necessarily lessen as the daughter grows up and matures. The good news is that your recovery is not based on what your mother does or doesn't do. It is not based on whether or not your mother stops being critical and obsessed with your weight or her weight. You are in control of your recovery! You do not have to end up like your mother! You have the ability to break free from the pattern of your mother's faulty behavior.

My parents don't want to have anything to do with my eating disorder treatment. Can I still resolve issues in my past if they refuse to become involved?

Yes, you can, although it is unfortunate they have chosen not to become involved at this point in your life. Remember, your personal happiness is not dependent on them. You can forgive them without their even knowing or accepting it.

Release any expectation you may have of them running to you and begging your forgiveness for all the pain they've caused you. This may never happen. By giving up this expectation, you can begin the process of creating your own personal happiness, regardless of the level of participation of others.

My parents think I'm too thin and have put me in four different hospitals. Nothing seems to work. Why?

Your parents can't cure you; only you can do that. *You* must make the decision to be well. Additionally, it has been my experience that hospital settings are not always the most conducive to whole-person recovery. Often the whole-person approach is not in place, while there is a great deal of control over food and eating. Learning how to eat and handle food appropriately, in a realistic setting, is our recommended therapeutic approach.

I've just found out that my daughter has an eating disorder. I don't understand how this could have happened. What should I do now?

You must face the truth of your child's eating disorder, no matter how much you are tempted to want to minimize it or deny its existence. It will not just go away on its own. Your child will require professional help to overcome this disorder. Your child will also need your support and your honesty during recovery.

Read all you can. Ask questions. Be prepared to fight for your child, but recognize you cannot cure her. (I recommend an excellent book titled *When Your Child Has an Eating Disorder* by Abigail H. Natenshon.)

I've never felt very comfortable with religious things. Can I find healing from my eating disorder without the spiritual component?

I believe we are spiritual beings. An eating disorder wreaks havoc with that spiritual side of ourselves. An eating disorder promotes shame, guilt, and feelings of worthlessness. It creates an atmosphere of despair and lack of hope. It saps the strength from our very being. It crushes our soul. An eating disorder is, then, a spiritual destroyer.

As a result, it is necessary to seek spiritual renewal. The components of recovery—characteristics like forgiveness, grace, and acceptance—are spiritual in nature. I believe that God is the author of forgiveness, grace, and acceptance. It is not illogical, then, to seek his help in obtaining and using these characteristics for yourself in your recovery. This is only accomplished through a renewed relationship with God. While an eating disorder promotes shame, God loves us no matter what. While an eating disorder produces guilt, God removes it through the sacrifice of Christ. While an eating disorder promotes feelings of worthlessness, God reminds us that we are his beloved children and valuable to him beyond measure. Faith creates an atmosphere of expectation and hope. It refreshes our strength and rekindles our soul.

Through the power of God, recovery from an eating disorder can become a wellspring of understanding, empathy, strength, and maturity. I have been privileged to watch the spiritual transformation of those with eating disorders. They have not only moved beyond their disorders but have been able to use what they have learned on their healing journeys to enrich their lives and the lives of others.

FOOD FOR THOUGHT

Touching the Right Chord

As you have read over these questions, there were probably several that touched you more deeply than others. Take a moment to review the questions and make a note of any that were especially meaningful to you. Which ones were they, and why? Were the answers given the ones you expected? If so, why? If not, why not? How would you have wanted the answers to be framed?

Did any of the questions, and the subsequent answers, make you angry? Did they make you sad? Did any give you hope?

Take some time to really explore your reactions to these questions. Allow yourself to think of other questions. Write them down and then indicate how you will go about finding the answers for yourself.

IN THE RIGHT DIRECTION

YOU CAN DO IT

Over the course of my career as a counselor and nutritionist, I have worked with hundreds of anorexics and bulimics. I've struggled with, comforted, prayed for, and loved every one of them. I've seen people who had given up on themselves and their lives find it in their hearts to try just one more time. I've seen them fight for their lives and win. I've also seen some lose.

I have been privileged to see the human spirit at its best and have had to endure accounts of humanity at its worst. Through all of that, one thing has remained clear to me: the remarkable strength of will that people possess to overcome their heartaches and to turn tragedy into triumph.

This future is possible for you. I know because I've seen it happen to others who, like you, were destroying themselves through eating disorders. I've seen them come to grips with the pain of their pasts. I've watched as they begin to treat their bodies as something special, giving them the care and nutrition they deserve. I've seen the miracle of spiritual awakening in souls thought long dead, and I've experienced through them their joy at rekindled relationships.

AFFIRMING ACTION

The road you are traveling is one taken by many others I've had the privilege to know and work with. They, like you, had their rough spots and flat stretches. Those who have reached their destination of health urge you to keep going. I urge you to keep going. The road to healing is so very worth the journey.

You now identify yourself by your disorder. Please know this is not the promise of your future. Wholeness lies beyond—a life without the constant identifying behavior of your disorder. You must want that life. You must commit to doing whatever it takes to reach for it. And once you have reached for it, you must determine never to let go.

I am behind you. God is with you.

Eating Disorder Questionnaire

The following list of questions will help you determine whether you or someone you know has an eating disorder. These questions are used in my counseling practice to help determine the type and severity of an eating disorder and also to spark discussion and dialogue among those with eating disorders and those who care for them. Even if you think you already know everything you need to know about an eating disorder, take the time to read them anyway. They may help solidify information or confirm an idea you've developed through personal experience or through reading this book.

Make your answers as honest as possible. Take all the time necessary to really think about each question before answering. (Be aware that some of the questions require you to be sitting down, ready to eat, before answering. It is fine to go ahead and read over these questions initially, but wait to answer them until you are prepared to eat.)

For those with access to the Internet, you can go to our Web site at www.aplaceofhope.com to take this questionnaire online. It will be automatically tabulated, and you will have an opportunity to send a message to us at The Center along with the results.

RELATIONSHIP TO FOOD AND EATING

Before eating, ask yourself the following questions:

- Why am I eating?
  - Hunger?

- ◆ Anger?
- ◆ Frustration?
- ◆ To fit into a group?
- ◆ To nourish my body?
- ◆ Other:
- • Why am I eating this particular food?
  - ◆ I like it?
  - ◆ It's handy?
  - ◆ Just to please someone else? Who?
  - ◆ It smells good?
  - ◆ It tastes good?
  - ◆ I think it's good for me?
  - ◆ It's *not* good for me?
  - ◆ Other:
- • What would I rather have?
- • Why am I eating here?
  - ◆ I feel relaxed here?
  - ◆ I like the people I'm with?
  - ◆ The atmosphere is pleasant?
  - ◆ The conversation is pleasant?
  - ◆ Other:
- • How could my experience be better?

While you are eating, ask yourself these questions:
- • Am I really enjoying this meal?
  - ◆ Am I tasting the food?
  - ◆ Am I feeling the texture of the food?
  - ◆ Am I distracted by things going on around me?
  - ◆ Am I paying attention to this food at all?
- • How does this food feel in my stomach?

- What do I feel, now that I'm eating?
  - Satisfaction?
  - Panic?
  - Guilt?
  - Other:
- Am I still eating after my hunger is satisfied? Why?

After eating, ask yourself the following questions:
- What aspects of this meal did I enjoy?
- How do I feel now that the food is part of me?
- If I'm still unsatisfied even though I'm full, why?
- Reasons why I am going to allow myself the time my body needs to rest and digest this food:

By sitting down and going over the reasons why you eat and what you feel during and after eating, you can pinpoint areas where problems still exist for you. If you are eating for any other reason than normal feelings of hunger, food has taken on an inappropriate place in your life, and you need to find out why. The next set of yes/no questions is designed to help you discover those reasons. If you answer yes to a question, indicate how often this happens.
- Do you have uncontrollable urges to eat until you become physically ill?
- Do you have episodes where you eat an enormous amount of food in a short period of time?
- Do you eat large amounts of food even when you're not hungry?
- Do you intentionally plan to eat alone in order to avoid questions regarding your eating?
- Do you feel guilty, depressed, or repulsed by how much you've eaten?
- Do you make yourself vomit to get rid of the food you've eaten?
- Is it hard to eat normal meals, without bingeing and purging?

- Do you use laxatives to control your weight or to get rid of food?
- Do you spit out food after chewing it to keep the food from getting into your stomach?
- Do you use diet pills to control your weight?
- Do you use water pills to control your weight? Exercise? Fasting? Enemas? Fad diets?
- Do you restrict the amount of calories you eat to control your weight?
- Are you preoccupied with what you eat?
- Are you constantly on a diet?
- Are you unwilling to gain weight in order to stop any faulty eating pattern you might have?

If you eat when you're not hungry, choose the following reasons that are most common for you:

- I'm bored.
- I'm lonely.
- I'm anxious.
- I'm stressed.
- It makes me feel good.
- The food I choose tastes good.
- No one else is around.
- Because the food is there.
- Because it's an established mealtime (breakfast, lunch, dinner).
- Because others around me are eating.
- Because I want to relax.
- Because I like to eat when I read.
- Because I like to eat when I'm watching television.
- Because I like to eat when I'm on the computer.
- I don't really know.

COADDICTIONS

Look over the following list of possible coaddictions and note any you are having trouble with. If you are experiencing "no use" with that substance, place a number 1 to the side. If you use the substance occasionally, write in a number 2. Write 3 if you use the substance to cope with unpleasant situations or emotions, and write 4 if your use is continual and compulsive.

1 = No use
2 = Occasional use
3 = Coping-mechanism use
4 = Compulsive use

_____Alcohol	_____Tranquilizers
_____Amphetamines	_____Cocaine
_____Antidepressants	_____Cigarettes
_____Barbiturates	_____Television
_____Hallucinogens	_____Shopping
(LSD, MDA, PCP)	_____Shoplifting
_____Marijuana	_____Gambling
_____Hashish	_____Sexual Activity

In all probability, you did not put a number 4 next to all of these addictions. If, however, you are using even a small percentage of these substances or habits in conjunction with your eating disorder, you have a compounded problem. To solve it, you'll need to develop a plan to address your other coaddictions.

FEELINGS

Read over the following statements about yourself, and circle "Agree" if that statement accurately reflects the way you feel. Circle "Disagree" if the statement isn't true for you. Circle "Don't Know" if you aren't sure of the relevancy of the statement.

Agree	Disagree	Don't Know	• I don't know how I feel inside.
Agree	Disagree	Don't Know	• I'm terrified of gaining weight.
Agree	Disagree	Don't Know	• The demands of adulthood are overwhelming.
Agree	Disagree	Don't Know	• The best years of my life happened when I was a child.
Agree	Disagree	Don't Know	• I feel alone in the world.
Agree	Disagree	Don't Know	• My relationships are not satisfying.
Agree	Disagree	Don't Know	• I feel I must do things perfectly or not at all.
Agree	Disagree	Don't Know	• I feel I am not in control of my life and how I eat.
Agree	Disagree	Don't Know	• I feel others expect excellence of me.
Agree	Disagree	Don't Know	• I feel guilty after eating too much.
Agree	Disagree	Don't Know	• I feel dissatisfied with the shape of my body.
Agree	Disagree	Don't Know	• I feel inadequate.
Agree	Disagree	Don't Know	• I have difficulty expressing how I feel.
Agree	Disagree	Don't Know	• I often feel empty inside.
Agree	Disagree	Don't Know	• I wish I were someone else.
Agree	Disagree	Don't Know	• I feel fat.
Agree	Disagree	Don't Know	• People would reject me if they knew the "real" me.
Agree	Disagree	Don't Know	• I cannot enjoy my accomplishments.
Agree	Disagree	Don't Know	• I feel ashamed to eat in the presence of other people.
Agree	Disagree	Don't Know	• I feel I am a worthless person.

| Agree | Disagree | Don't Know | • I feel I cannot live up to the expectations of others. |
| Agree | Disagree | Don't Know | • I do not feel comfortable in social situations. |

If you have agreed with even a few of these statements, your self-esteem is in need of renewal. Go back over those statements you answered "Agree" to and think about *why* you feel that way and *who* you might have received that message from.

If you answered "Don't Know" to any statements, go back and really think about that statement again. Your response could be coming from the numbing effect of your disorder.

AFFIRMING ACTION

By now you've probably understood that getting to know yourself, your body, and who you are is vital to your healing. It's essential for your recovery, and it's going to remain essential for the rest of your life.

So many people in this world stop discovering who they are. They allow other people, other things, and other influences to identify them as people. Through the course of your journey, you'll be learning to keep track of your current self-image and how it's progressing.

Your eating disorder has been covering up the real you. Now that you're rediscovering yourself, keep up the progress. One of the natural offshoots of growth is change. That process will not stop once you've reached your goal of health.

Please go online to www.aplaceofhope.com/audio/
selfdiscovery.html for my special message
on continuing your journey of self-discovery.

By now, you've had one or two surprises concerning who you are as a person. Expect more. Your eating disorder needs to stop, but your personal growth need never end. Up to this point, you've been diverting time and energy toward your eating disorder that can now be used toward your continuing self-discovery. Expect change! Embrace life!

Resource List

The following resources are provided to assist you on your healing journey. This is by no means an exhaustive list of the materials available on eating disorders, but I have found each resource to be of value in my treatment of people with eating disorders.

If there were one resource I would place above all others, it is the Bible. God, as our Creator, is the ultimate source of our understanding who we are and what we need. Many of the resources listed below include a spiritual component to the questions posed and answers given. May God provide you insight as you seek greater understanding of yourself and of him.

BOOKS

Addiction and Grace: Love and Spirituality in the Healing of Addictions by Gerald G. May, M.D., Harper San Francisco, 1988. This conversational-style book is a concise discussion of the need for grace in our lives. I found pages 24-34 very meaningful, especially pages 31-32 on "security addictions."

The Adonis Complex: The Secret Crisis of Male Body Obsession by Harrison G. Pope, Jr., M.D., Katharine A. Phillips, M.D., and Roberto Olivardia, Ph.D., The Free Press/Simon and Schuster, 2000. More and more men are becoming susceptible to obsessive and faulty body image. This amazing book looks at body dysmorphism from the male point of view. On pages 142-143 of chapter 6, "Fear of Fat: Men and Eating Disorders," there is an excellent list of clues that can be used to help someone determine whether or not he has an eating disorder.

The Adult Children of Alcoholics Syndrome by Wayne Kritsberg, Bantam Books, 1985. This classic book outlines the adult characteristics of children of alcoholics. Many of these characteristics are common to eating disorders.

All Your Health Questions Answered Naturally by Maureen Kennedy Salaman, MKS, Inc., 1998. This thick, comprehensive book is an absolute must for those interested in answers and solutions that take a "natural" approach to health issues. This book is for everyone!

The Amazing Connection Between Love and Food by Dr. Gary Smalley, Tyndale, 2001. This marvelous book really targets food and relationships. It looks at how foods affect relationships and how relationships affect your health.

The Bible Cure for Weight Loss and Muscle Gain: Ancient Truths, Natural Remedies and the Latest Findings for Your Health Today by Don Colbert, M.D., Siloam Press, 2000. This compact book can fit into many back pockets and purses, yet it's packed with solid biblical answers. Especially helpful is chapter 5, "Power for Change Through Faith in God."

BioMarkers: The 10 Keys to Prolonging Vitality by William Evans, Ph.D., and Irwin H. Roseberg, M.D., with Jacqueline Thompson, Simon and Schuster, 1991. The authors are professors of nutrition and medicine at Tufts University. This book looks at ten specific "bio-markers" to optimize health and vitality for all ages.

The Broken Mirror: Understanding and Treating Body Dysmorphic Disorder by Katharine A. Phillips, M.D., Oxford University Press, 1986. This groundbreaking book gives a name to an obsession with perceived physical flaws: body dysmorphic disorder. It is a blend of compelling real-life stories and cutting-edge psychological research.

Boundaries by Dr. Henry Cloud and Dr. John Townsend, Zondervan, 1992. This book is an excellent presentation of physical, mental, emotional, and spiritual boundaries, from a well-balanced and spiritual point of view.

The Carbohydrate Addict's Healthy Heart Program: Break Your Carbo-Insulin Connection to Heart Disease by Dr. Richard F. Heller, Dr. Rachael F. Heller, and Dr. Frederic J. Vagnini, Ballantine, 1999. For those seeking new patterns of eating that will assist in making healthy food choices, this book provides some wonderful information and charts, especially the "Low-Carbohydrate Foods List" on pages 132-133 of chapter 5.

Conquering Depression: A 3-Day Plan to Finding Happiness by Mark A. Sutton and Bruce Hennigan, M.D., Broadman and Holman, 2001. This book includes some wonderful sections in each chapter under the headings "Strength for Today" and "Tools for Tomorrow." It also includes thirty tear-apart reminder cards at the back of the book called "Life Filters."

Father Hunger by Robert S. McGee, Vine Books/Servant, 1993. This book is a look at the void left in a woman's heart without a healthy relationship with her father, a void that is often filled by food. I found chapter 14, "Mental Snapshots of the Past," to have some excellent material on the emotional connection between fathers and daughters.

Food Addiction: The Body Knows by Kay Sheppard, Health Communications, 1989. Although written in the late 1980s, when the concept of food addiction was becoming more accepted, this is still a very helpful book, especially chapter 3, "The Progression of Food Addiction."

Food and Love by Dr. Gary Smalley, Tyndale, 2001. Gary Smalley looks at how food affects relationships and how food affects health. An excellent book with insights for eating better and strengthening your ability to love well.

Food and Mood: The Complete Guide to Eating Well and Feeling Your Best by Elizabeth Somer, M.A., R.D., Henry Holt and Company, 1995. This is a great resource that gives valuable information on cravings, nutrition, eating disorders, and mental functioning.

Healing the Shame That Binds You by John Bradshaw, Health Communications, 1988. In chapter 3, "The Hiding Places of Toxic Shame," Bradshaw goes over such characteristics as perfectionism, striving for power and control, rage, criticism and blame, and people-pleasing—all of which have special significance in eating disorders.

Hope Again: When Life Hurts and Dreams Fade by Charles R. Swindoll, Word, 1996. This is a buoyant book offering hope even in the midst of pain. Chapter 2, "Hope Beyond Suffering," includes some wonderful insights on how to rejoice through hard times.

The Hope and Healing Subscription Series by Dr. Gregory Jantz. Order a yearly subscription and receive an audiotape every month to support your recovery. Each tape is approximately one hour long, during which Dr. Jantz shares on such topics as how others have overcome the desire to binge, the traits of women who achieve long-term recovery from eating disorders, and learning to make food safe again. (These tapes are not intended as a substitute for counseling or treatment.) Available at www.aplaceofhope.com.

How Did This Happen? A Practical Guide to Understanding Eating Disorders— for Teachers, Parents and Coaches by the Institute for Research and Education, HealthSystem Minnesota, 1999. This booklet is an introductory overview designed for the specific groups mentioned in the title. As such, it is not comprehensive but does answer some basic questions about eating disorders.

How People Grow: What the Bible Reveals About Personal Growth by Dr. Henry Cloud and Dr. John Townsend, Zondervan, 2001. Recovery from an eating disorder presents tremendous opportunity for personal growth.

I found chapter 4, "The God of Grace," especially moving. I love the line that opens the chapter: "People must discover that God is for them and not against them." This is such a fundamental truth for those with eating disorders.

How to Be a Happy, Healthy Family by Jim Burns, Ph.D., Word, 2001. This book outlines the ten principles of families that succeed and can be used to learn and strengthen healthy parenting patterns.

The Key to Your Child's Heart by Dr. Gary Smalley, Word, 1992. This classic book, on bestseller lists for fifteen years, begins with a presentation of the "major destroyers" of families, such as "a closed spirit," "refusing to forgive," and "84 ways you can offend your children." These major destroyers may be factors in the formation of eating disorders.

Like Mother, Like Daughter: How Women Are Influenced by Their Mother's Relationship with Food—and How to Break the Pattern by Debra Waterhouse, M.Ph., R.D., Hyperion, 1997. This book frankly discusses the link between mothers and their daughters' relationship with food. It's a very worthwhile read, though not an easy one.

The Link Between A.D.D. and Addiction: Getting the Help You Deserve by Wendy Richardson, M.A., Piñon Press, 1997. At first glance, this book may not appear to have much to offer regarding eating disorders; however, it provides information on anorexia, binge eating, bulimia, compulsive overeating, self-medicating with food, and sugar addiction.

Love and Its Counterfeits by Barbara Cook, Aglow, 1989. Healthy relationships are essential for mending the damage done by an eating disorder. This book assists readers in distinguishing between genuine love and its many counterfeits.

Mom, I Feel Fat! Becoming Your Daughter's Ally in Developing a Healthy Body Image by Sharon A. Hersh, Shaw, 2001. This book answers the question,

"How can I raise a healthy daughter in a culture that worships thinness and exalts appearance?" Written specifically with mothers in mind, it challenges you to really think about your own self-image and be proactive in helping your daughter develop hers.

New Hope for Binge Eaters: Advances in the Understanding and Treatment of Bulimia by Harrison G. Pope Jr., M.D., and James I. Hudson, M.D., Harper and Row, 1984. This book is geared specifically toward bulimia and includes some excellent self-administered personal inventories, including the one titled "Bulimia-Associated Disorders Quiz" on page 40 of chapter 4.

Nutrition and Mental Illness: An Orthomolecular Approach to Balancing Body Chemistry by Carl C. Pfeiffer, Ph.D., M.D., Healing Arts Press, 1987. Don't let the title of this book throw you. This book explores Dr. Pfeiffer's work in the connection between nutrition and mental illness, from anxiety and depression to phobias and schizophrenia and bipolar disorder. Chapter 5, "B_6 and Zinc—The Missing Link," is especially relevant to those with eating disorders.

Potatoes Not Prozac: A Natural Seven-Step Dietary Plan to Control Your Cravings and Lose Weight, Recognize How Foods Affect the Way You Feel, and Stabilize the Level of Sugar in Your Blood by Kathleen DesMaisons, Ph.D., Simon and Schuster, 1998. I love the title of this book! The information on blood sugar levels, as they relate to eating disorders, is vital in understanding the physical nature of eating disorders.

Raising Great Kids: A Comprehensive Guide to Parenting with Grace and Truth by Dr. Henry Cloud and Dr. John Townsend, Zondervan, 1999. This enormously helpful book outlines deliberate steps parents can take to give their children the love and support they deserve. Because so many eating disorders evolve out of a breakdown in parent-child relationships, this book can help those with eating disorders to avoid the shortcomings of their own upbringing. Especially helpful is the concept of "connectedness" outlined in chapter 4, "Laying the Foundation of Life."

Real Solutions for Forgiving the Unforgivable by David Stoop, Vine Books/Servant, 2001. Part of the Real Solutions series, this small but powerful book explores the various themes around forgiveness. Chapter 6, "The Path of Forgiveness," is especially helpful.

The Serotonin Solution: The Potent Brain Chemical That Can Help You Stop Bingeing, Lose Weight, and Feel Great by Judith J. Wurtman, Ph.D. and Susan Suffes, Fawcett Columbine/Ballantine, 1996. This book starts with a discussion of "Why We Overeat" and examines the concept of food as tranquilizer. It includes specific food and meal recommendations for different types of common stresses, as well as "The Serotonin Seeker's Diet," based on the author's research at M.I.T.

The Soul Care Bible edited by Tim Clinton, Nelson, 2001. This Bible is an excellent spiritual resource for those recovering from an eating disorder or other addiction. There are special sections devoted to recovery, including eating disorders.

What's Real, What's Ideal: Overcoming a Negative Body Image by Brangien Davis, Rosen, 1999. Written especially for adolescents, this book is part of the Teen Health Library of Eating Disorder Prevention. Other titles in this series are *Anorexia Nervosa: When Food Is the Enemy, Eating Disorder Survivors Tell Their Stories,* and *Exercise Addiction: When Fitness Becomes an Obsession.*

What the Bible Says About Healthy Living: Three Biblical Principles That Will Change Your Diet and Improve Your Health by Rex Russell, M.D., Regal, 1996. Dr. Russell defines these principles as: (1) eat the foods God created for you, (2) don't alter God's design, and (3) don't let any food or drink become your god.

When Your Child Has an Eating Disorder: A Step-by-Step Workbook for Parents and Other Caregivers by Abigail H. Natenshon, Jossey-Bass, 1999. This workbook is written for parents of preteen through college-age children. Chapter 2, "Recognizing the Signs of Disease," is especially helpful.

Working with Emotional Intelligence by Daniel Goleman, Bantam, 1998. While this is not a book specifically targeted for those with eating disorders, it provides practical real-life stories and solutions of how individuals deal with triumphs, disasters, and dramatic turnarounds. Chapter 4, "The Inner Rudder," gives a fascinating presentation of how to recognize one's emotions and their effects.

The Yeast Connection: A Medical Breakthrough by William G. Crook, M.D., Vintage Books, 1986. The information in this book is crucial for those who desire to understand the role yeast and yeast infections have on eating disorders.

BOOKS BY DR. GREGORY L. JANTZ

21 Days to Better Eating, Zondervan, 1998.

Becoming Strong Again, Revell/Baker, 1998.

Healing the Scars of Emotional Abuse, Revell/Baker, 1995.

Hidden Dangers of the Internet, Harold Shaw, 1998.

Losing Weight Permanently: The Secrets of the 2% Who Succeed, Harold Shaw, 1996.

Recupera Tu Salud Emocional (Spanish-language edition of *Becoming Strong Again*), Panorama, 1999.

The Spiritual Path to Weight Loss, Publications International, 1997.

Too Close to the Flame: Recognizing and Avoiding Sexualized Relationships,
Howard, 1999.

Turning the Tables on Gambling: Hope and Help for an Addictive Behavior,
Harold Shaw, 2000.

INTERNET RESOURCES

Anorexia Nervosa and Related Eating Disorders, Inc.: www.anred.com

The Center for Counseling and Health Resources, Inc.:
www.aplaceofhope.com

National Eating Disorders Association: www.nationaleatingdisorders.org

International Association of Eating Disorder Professionals: www.iaedp.com

National Association of Anorexia Nervosa and Associated Disorders:
www.anad.org

Other Important Sites

www.caringonline.com. General information, news, and resource and
referral information are maintained here as an outreach of Dr. Jantz
and The Center, Inc.

www.humanville.com. Cynthia French's homepage.

www.something-fishy.org. The owner of this large Web site with many
resources is a recovered anorexic who provides the site as a service to
those seeking information and help.

Notes

CHAPTER THREE: WHEN FAMILIES UNRAVEL

1. Wayne Kritsberg, *The Adult Children of Alcoholics Syndrome* (New York: Bantam, 1985), 30.

CHAPTER FOUR: THE HIDDEN SHADOW OF ABUSE

1. I outline this process in detail in *Healing the Scars of Emotional Abuse* (Grand Rapids, Mich.: Baker, 1995).

CHAPTER FIVE: THE ADDICTION OF CHOICE

1. Wendy Richardson, *The Link Between A.D.D. and Addiction* (Colorado Springs, Colo.: Piñon Press, 1997), 35.

CHAPTER SIX: THE DETOUR OF DENIAL

1. Dr. Jim Burns, *How to Be a Happy, Healthy Family* (Nashville: Word, 2001), 114-7.

CHAPTER EIGHT: MAKING YOUR BODY YOUR FRIEND

1. The name-brand eating disorder formulas I recommend throughout this book are either supplements that I have personally helped to develop or formulas that I have used with success over a long period of time. Call toll-free 1-888-771-5166 for more information.

2. Adapted from Dr. William G. Crook, *The Yeast Connection* (New York: Vintage, 1986), 7.

CHAPTER THIRTEEN: HEALING AS A JOURNEY

1. Gary Smalley, *The Amazing Connection Between Food and Love* (Wheaton, Ill.: Tyndale, 2001), 171.

CHAPTER SIXTEEN: LEARNING TO LIVE

1. Anne Frank, *Anne Frank: The Diary of a Young Girl, the Definitive Edition,* ed. Otto H. Frank and Mirjam Pressler, trans. Susan Massotty (New York: Doubleday, 1995), 281.

About the Authors

Gregory L. Jantz, Ph.D., is a popular speaker and award-winning author. He is a certified chemical dependency professional, a nationally certified psychologist, and a certified eating disorder specialist. Dr. Jantz is the founder and executive director of The Center for Counseling and Health Resources, Inc., a leading mental health and chemical dependency treatment facility with three clinics in the Seattle, Washington, area.

The Center for Counseling and Health Resources, specializing in whole-person care, is a full-service counseling center, and a referral and information source for those seeking help for eating disorders. Individuals from across the world come to The Center to participate in the hope-filled work of recovery from addictive behaviors. Dr. Jantz's whole-person approach to eating disorders addresses the emotional, relational, intellectual, physical, and spiritual dimensions of each person with a unique, tailored treatment plan. Over the course of the past eighteen years, Dr. Jantz and The Center have treated nearly seven thousand people, with all types of eating disorders, using the successful whole-person approach.

Dr. Jantz speaks nationally at conferences, seminars, and retreats on a wide variety of topics, utilizing his extensive expertise and experience. Dr. Jantz has also hosted several popular live call-in radio shows, participating in well over a thousand individual interviews since 1995. He is the author of numerous books, including *Healing the Scars of Emotional Abuse, Losing Weight Permanently: Secrets of the 2% Who Succeed, The Spiritual Path to Weight Loss, 21 Days to Eating Better, Becoming Strong Again, Hidden Dangers of the Internet, Too Close to the Flame: Recognizing and Avoiding Sexualized Relationships,* and *Turning the Tables on Gambling: Hope and Help for an Addictive Behavior.*

Dr. Jantz hosts the Hope Series, a monthly audiotape club on the topic of eating disorders. This resource is sent monthly to subscribers across the United States and provides cutting-edge nutritional information, new advances in the treatment of eating disorders, inspiration to aid healing, and practical suggestions for ongoing recovery.

Dr. Jantz and his wife, LaFon, have been married for eighteen years. They have two sons, Gregg and Benjamin.

Ann McMurray is a freelance writer living in Mountlake Terrace, Washington. Ann and her husband, Tad, have been married for twenty-four years and have two children, Joel and Lindsay.

Ann has worked with Dr. Jantz on *Hope, Help and Healing for Eating Disorders, Healing the Scars of Emotional Abuse, Hidden Dangers of the Internet, Too Close to the Flame,* and *Turning the Tables on Gambling.* Her partnership with Dr. Jantz extends to The Center where she works as an operations assistant. She is also the point of contact for much of the communication coming from The Center's Web site at **www.aplaceofhope.com** and The Center's news and information Web site at **www.caringonline.com.**

For more information about resources related to eating disorders, or to speak to someone about eating disorders, please call The Center toll-free at **1-888-771-5166.** You may also contact The Center at **www.aplaceofhope.com** for more information about The Center, to sign up for the Eating Disorder Newsletter, to sign up for the Hope Series audiotapes, or to receive information about speaking engagements with Dr. Jantz. The Center, Inc., can also be contacted by mail at **P.O. Box 700, Edmonds, WA 98020.**